Also by the Author

Cor Meum Poetry, Poetry of My Heart
Cor Meum Redux, Poetry of My Heart Revisited
The Rest of Me

Thinking Straight

W. RICHARD PATTERSON

THINKING STRAIGHT

iUniverse books may be ordered through booksellers or by contacting:

iUniverse
1663 Liberty Drive
Bloomington, IN 47403
www.iuniverse.com
844-349-9409

ISBN: 978-1-6632-5283-8 (sc)
ISBN: 978-1-6632-5282-1 (e)

Library of Congress Control Number: 2023908926

Print information available on the last page.

iUniverse rev. date: 05/11/2023

Front cover artwork by the author-Thinking Straight
acrylic on canvas.

CONTENTS

INTRODUCTION

In writing this, my diminutive Magnus Opus, I have striven to keep things simple. There are no deep philosophical thoughts or reasonings, just the desire of a simple man trying to better understand his world.

There are many subjects explored and certainly none plumbed to any great depth. Just musings of an elder man trying to understand better the going on's around him. It has become evident to me we are all in one sense petty thieves. Writers take ideas, thoughts and words from other writers without any attributions. Artists take from other artists, science from science, and nations from nations. Often times this is done unconsciously or without intent. Thats just how we humans operate. Nothing new under the sun, I suppose, there is not an original thought among us. An honest person is one who acknowledges their indebtedness to others. At some level we all seem content to drift along in the warm waters of hypocrisy. As a hypocrite, I can easily spot a fellow hypocrite be it a Black Lives Matter activist who lives in palatial homes in safe upscale neighborhoods all the while preaching racial discord. We observe Uber rich portly ex-Vice Presidents jetting around with fellow carnival barkers lecturing us on supposedly rising sea levels and hypothetical man made climate change which the rest of us simply call normal climate change.

We as a nation are so divided now as we yell past each other trying to be heard above the din. Even being disparate people groups, we are still united as a nation, an American nation. There is still room in the public square for healthy debate and dialog. This is my hope for this book; tell me your opinions that we might have a gracious conversations.

However, I have learned this is not always possible and actually may not be sought after. At this point, I have learned from wise little sister Sue, there are times to build walls. Robert Frost had much to say about fences and another stated, before you tear down a wall, it is best to know why it was erected in the first place. When people become so toxic, vitriolic and at times hateful, this is the time to construct a chain link type fence even festooned with razor wire which still allows the possibility to see through and talk to each other. But, these people are not allowed to enter my space and disrupt my peace. Maybe we can resolve our differences as we talk and learn about each other through the fence. The other type of wall is a brick wall. These people do not need to be seen or heard. This place is inhabited by rank evil people who can only be redeemed by the Divine.

Join me as I discuss many various subjects and lets have a discussion.

CHAPTER 1

Thoughts

In musing and thinking upon my long life, it is with humility I recognize my thoughts are not original. There is no ephemeral moment when I realized I had stumbled onto a new idea or an original thought. Even with a superficial pondering, it becomes obvious that king Solomon was quite accurate in his summation that there is nothing new under the sun. There are few polymaths in any generation: rare is the Isaac Newton, Leonardo da Vinci or a Blaisé Pascal. True genius is nurtured and brought forward by patience. Patience to think and create. Of course, pure genius can be manifested by frenzied activity; but who really knows whats in the mind of a Mozart or a Beethoven? There is almost a type of madness that finds it's release in creativity.

We hurry along, afraid or unwilling to slow down, to think. We have great difficulty living in the present as we long for the future; lamenting it's slow arrival or recall the past trying to slow it's inevitable departure. This results in man wandering about in times that do not belong to him as he seldom thinks of the now.

So, there is no genius or madness in the notation and summation of my musings. As my sister Sue remarked once, "Everything Richard knows he has read in a book." This is, of course, quite true; but an incomplete sentiment. Climbing upon the shoulders of great people allows one to gaze farther than if left to our own possible weak mentation.

This is the way it should be; there is no need trying to reinvent the wheel, be it the Buddhist Wheel of Life or any other type wheel. This is a fools errand. Collecting thoughts and ideas from many hundreds of sources has enabled me to synthesize and amalgamate what I believe is important. It certainly is not the study of philosophy or pseudo-science masquerading as true repeatable theory tested science.

So much of what passes for knowledge is on closer scrutiny nothing more than opinion. Many today are lazy in their analysis going with the first reading or profess an understanding, but with a slight scratching of the veneer; a reflection of dull lead is seen, no glittering insights or true revelations, but only dullness which the lightly educated person might view as gospel; ergo, macro evolution, man's ascent, trans sexualism, man centric climate change and other endless nonsense. If I believed I had but one week to live, I am sure my passions would be rendered less intense, but eventually there comes a time when mythologies and philosophies become tiring. We tire of trees morphing into maidens of the forest or faries dancing in the vales; we long for more substance. There is always a yearning for simplicity not complexity. Simple life, hearth and home with little strife.

There are few quotes or references in this paper because it is not a peer reviewed document, but just knowledge that I have accumulated over decades of observing and studying human nature.

I realize, of course, not all who read about my thoughts will be inclined to my worldview, however; I must be true to myself and my conclusions. There is only one Truth and we all try to understand it in our own way. But our hearts are inclined toward error. Often we are incapable of seeing truth or reasoning well. In some ways, it might be better to know a little about everything, than everything about a little. As stated earlier, these subjects that are touched upon are my mere musings. No subject is explored in depth or examined exhaustively which I am sure would be beyond my capabilities. I tried to keep G.K. Chesterton, the great apostle of common sense in mind as I wrote down my thoughts. Simplicity and common sense should be my guide as I pursue the truth of these matters.

This paper I hope will avoid any trappings of a screed. The subjects covered are, I believe, well thought out ideas with subsequent sober conclusions. Again, I am claiming no expertise in any subject, but only a simple man using common sense trying to understand the world.

I will begin by asking the big question; how did we happen to find ourselves upon this sphere floating through space?

CHAPTER 2

Origins

Must I believe I am God or must I believe I am nothing? There must be a middle ground. I am hemmed in by a terrifying universe. As the Acts of the Apostles states, I am assigned one miniscule space at this particular time, knowing no rhyme nor reason why this is so. I am given this brief allotted time not really knowing what went before me for eternity or what will come after me for eternity. There is only infinity surrounding this fleeting moment. I know there is no evasion but only death coming for me of which I know nothing about. Indeed, I am like an icy cold worm, an oscillating atom floating in space, but I have this sense that Somebody knows my name keeping me from utter dispair. The overwhelming sense is that the universe has an aim and purpose which must speak to an Author.

The Big Bang model does not fully explain the origin of the universe since it cannot explain how time, space and energy came to be. If there was a Big Bang, there had to be a Big Banger. This model describes a universe coming into existance from an ultra dense and high temperature initial state.

Of course science has much to say about the origin of the universe with many theories proffered. The great mathematicians, physicists, students of the cosmos and others have contributed immeasurably to our knowledge. Where would we be without the great minds of Kepler, Copernicus, Newton, Heisenberg, Einstein to name a few. But we must remember science itself has a half life; it is forever changing and often contradicts itself. This is as it should be, it needs to continually be tested and reexamined. Any consensus concerning science must be viewed with suspicion. We have the uncanny ability to describe something in greater detail than we can explain. The more we probe into the unknown, the more it should humble us directing us to Socrates wisdom of "I know nothing." The physics, the constants, the mathematics are fixed as if by a Great Maker, The Ultimate Thinker, The Supreme Watchmaker, a Mind that knows all possible things knowable and unknowable; of course; Yahweh, God of the Hebrew and Christian Scriptures.

In spite of the 10th to the 70th or even 10th to the 700th power chance that the universe just came into existance de novo at a singular moment; much like a hard drive in a computer, it still requires software programming to function. This then begs the question, if a program, who is the programmer? 10th to the 70th power or 10th to the 700th power are nonsense numbers that don't exist. This alone should argue against our vaunted theories.

We know Newtonian physics is correct as we know quantum mechanic physics is correct. However, they are incompatible with each other, but nevertheless, the universe just keeps humming along regardless of this mighty paradox. This creates a conundrum of great complexity tasking the keen minds to find a unifying theory of everything and the elusive "God" particle. Einstein spent the latter part of his life trying to find and harmonize a theory of everything. He of course, along with all others, have failed in trying to unify multiple disparate theories.

We have learned so much we have boxed ourselves inside an impenetrable, maddening maze. But, we press on using more imaginative language, sophisticated jargon with dizzing formulas trying to explain the unexplainable. We have little understanding of dark matter or early dark matter. With the Hubble telescope or the Webb telescope peering deeply into the universe, we still cannot scientifically explain the origin of the universe. Many will not bend a knee to the concept of a Creator God, which would explain all we need to know about creation.

The origin of the universe, life and man are shrouded in mystery. It is impossible for us to know how the world was created anymore than we could create it. Considering eternity and my truncated time here on this globe, I must wonder why I am here now and who put me here, much like the proverbial turtle atop a fence post. Certainly not some cosmic accident did this. Even as a humorous joke, it wears thin. And when I do laugh, it reminds me that only man is imbued with laughter. There is some greatness albeit small in knowing you are not the reason for the universe.

CHAPTER 3

Evolution

We are not the product of evolution. Of course, micro evolution exists, we can see this all the time; a bird or a moth might change their coloration over time, but they still remain a bird or a moth. Macro evolution is what entangles the Rationalist Evolutionist in absurdum reductum arguments. Nobody is able to envision something originating from nothingness. The very thought of absolute nothingness staggers the mind. The best we can conjure when thinking of nothingness is a vacuum or a void. However, both are not completely empty; they contain time and force fields whose origins remain entirely unknown.

Saint Augustine of Hippo had something to say about time. God created time, it didn't exist before He created it. It is right there in Genesis 1:1, "in the beginning God created." Eternity is different from time. God is before time and also at the end of time; eternity outside of time. So just the cavalier attitude about time in our thinking and understanding has a certain air of hubris about it. We talk about creation and evolution happening over many billions of years not realizing that the marking of these events were measured in time, which is a construct of God. How humorous is Augustine's response to the question, "what was God doing before creating earth?" The answer being, "preparing Hell for people who pry into mysteries."

Evolution is a strange idea. Of course, we can all agree that the fittest survive as we see all the fit plants and animals surrounding us. Our understanding concerning evolution consists mainly in missing links with copious assumptions and speculations. The Big Bang model actually creates more problems for the evolutionist than it does for the creationists.

Even if I did not believe in a Creator and agreed with the evolutionist that life began when amino acids were activated by lightening and joined together against all mathematical odds creating a single strand of basic amino acids, my statement then would be "wonderful, now do it again and again and again." Creating life is really quite more than this primitive model. Scientist with their inexhaustable hubris and condensensions are always amazing.

We can all imagine a fish surviving a flood, but maybe not so much an elephant. We might have to wait for a very long time to see if the elephant ever changes into a fish. We can all imagine a man drawing a picture of any animal for example, of a monkey, but we cannot imagine a monkey ever drawing the likeness of a man. All monkeys for all time laboring together at their typewriters could never randomly reproduce the works of Shakespeare's million words.

We are different from all other creatures including angels, as far as we know, in the fact that we can create. Man is a co-creator much like his Creator which follows from the logic of the Imago Dei.

From abortion to zydeco music and an alphabet of possibilities in-between, man is a queer animal. However, if we can see him truly as an animal is when he can be seen to be more, much more. The more we examine him as an animal, the less he will appear to be one. He is first and foremost a product of a marvelous revolution, not the spawn of random oscillating pools of primordial soup.

But we are indeed a paradox, so vile on the one hand that we not only fashion an idol of a beast, but will also bow down to worship it. We are marvelous one moment, a monster the next, the refuse and the glory of the universe, a wavering reed, a granite plinth, a rebellious vice-regent of the universe. However, man through grace is like unto God, the Divine Imago Dei; without grace a beast of the field (Prov. 3:31, Joel 2:28, Eccl 3:1, 8).

One branch of the ugly is the beautiful; with beauty often being in the eyes of the beholder. Even the most ignorant among us knows when viewing life we have forgotten heaven. Nature created by God is a great signature work demonstrating His Omnipotence and our quaking smallness which will forever hide infinity from us.

I should know myself better, thus, making it beneficial for me as I take charge of my thoughts. This longing, this knowing, hopefully will lead me to wisdom which will then lead me back to my innocent childhood, (except as ye become as little children, Matt. 18:3). We must humbly remind ourselves that only God bestows wisdom, and the fear of God is the beginning of wisdom.

CHAPTER 4

———✺———

Nature

It is healing and life giving to be aware of the beauty, awe and wonderment of nature. The very universe speaks to the remarkable simplicity and complexity of this God created masterpiece. When logic and rhetoric fail in describing this wonderment, poetry comes forth. It might not be as precise as science, or as logical as we might desire, but at the same time it requires no apology, defense or persuasion. Great poets and artists have the gift of perceiving things with fresh eyes and deeper insight. Nature is a balm for the spirit while educating the soul. It can beguile us, charm us and inspire us as it has throughout the ages, but it cannot bore us. God is not only Love, He is also Beauty and certainly is not boring.

The fury of nature humbles us while instilling awe and fear. Our feeble attempts at explaining nature while trying to control or tame this marvel should humble us. It brought fear to the fishermen as Jesus slept in the boat. They knew weather, knowing it was beyond their control. In a panic they woke Him and He calmed the storm with a word. Of course, these men knew this was impossible with mere men; so they recognized they were in the presence of someone truly terrifying someone who controlled the storm, the God of the universe. My goodness this should give us pause.

When we view the earth and heavens, we know at a deep level something or Someone created it all. Of course, with our vaunted intellect we push back against the obvious; it's almost as if we can't help ourselves. The Apostle Paul spoke to this matter in his magisterial Book of Romans. "For since the creation of the world, His invisible attributes, His eternal power and divine nature, have been clearly seen, being understood through what has been made, so that they are without excuse. For even though they knew God, they did not honor Him as God, or give thanks, but they became futile in their speculations, and their foolish heart was darkened." Romans 1:20-21. That indeed is a profound statement.

Nature is forever changing, the change is inevitable: night gives way to day, Autumn seques into Winter. Somehow and we don't know how, the entire universe is connected. Each of us in our own time and place, each stone, each star, each puff of wind affects the entire. Blaisé Pascal understood this when he declared "The least movement is of importance to all nature. The entire ocean is affected by a pebble."

If we can realize all things do change, there really is nothing we can hold on to keeping it ourselves. This is a lesson I have long been coming to understand. Nothing lasts forever, not even the stars. As God states in His Book of Revelation; He will make all things new in the appointed time.

After many years of pondering and thinking upon the mysteries and heartbreak of change, there dawned moments of unexpected comprehensions only the poet could give meaning to. It actually is an eternal question; the question of why? Why am I here, now or for that matter at any time? My answer concerning the beauty and wonderment of Nature is summed up in the undefinable word Love. God is Love: therefore I am love. This feeling I am sure will be parsed as we marinate forever in His Goodness and inexhaustible Love. In the here and now, I need to nurture a quiet gratitude concerning my brief moment here not needing to know or understand why, but have this tender place for gratitude.

There is no doubt that God's nature is beautiful and awesome, however, man is also awesome and creative. Who but man would ever dream of building castles in the sky? No other life force can possess this wild imagination. Of course, other animals and even some plants can construct structures that should merit our praise and wonderment. Even Solomon in all his splendor was never arrayed with such beauty as the flowers of the field. The exquisite and often simple beauty of a particular beautiful bird or a stunning liquid sunset should be marveled at with attendant humility. The Bower bird's bowery, the maniacal dancing of the Manikans, or the outlandish siren attractions of the Birds of Paradise are almost beyond belief. Few can match musical lyrics of the Lyre Bird or the plantive call of the Common Loon. Even the symphonic arrangement on a summer eve with performances by tree frogs, pond frogs, the basso of the Bullfrog all accompanied by cicadis, crickets and the owls timely hoot cannot be minimized. Often a breeze rustles the leaves and wends its way through the trees lending a background canvas allowing all to paint a portrait.

No doubt but God's creation is awesome but He made us to be co-creators with Him with nothing matching the creative wonderment of man. The architecture of the great Cathedrals, palaces of powerful monarchs, the breathtaking pulchitrude of sea side villages or mountainous hamlets is not equaled by any builder but man. Beautiful paintings and sculptures cannot be matched by any lesser creature. There is not even a feeble attempt by any creature, but man in these endeavors.

We must pay deference to all the wonderful sounds in nature. However, none can even come close to the pure genius of music produced by man. From the soaring melodies of Rachmaninoff, the fabulous restrained cacophany of notes by young Mozart, brooding penetrating structures of incomparable Beethoven, the complex haunting melodies of Chopin, or the diminutive in stature only of Schuberts Leider songs, such as his Elkong with it's driving fearful music set to a Gothe poem; these will never be reproduced by nature.

It is fascinating to me that it appears to have been about a three hundred year period when such stupendous music was penned. Genius after genius wrote columns of meter and measure of timeless pieces. Any genera of music is to be appreciated be it Turkish guitar, Country music, Blues, Gospel, Hip Hop, if they represent their kind well. The structure of a simple melody, a well thought out sonata or the complexities of a concerto or symphony must be appreciated and can never be duplicated by any other living creature but man with all his attendant glory. In a future chapter, I will spend more time discussing the uniqueness of music and the arts.

But suffice it to say, we were created not only to enjoy the beauty of nature, but to create wonderment using our unique minds and hands. What a gift our maker has bestowed upon us, the Glory of the universe.

CHAPTER 5

———— ✺ ————

Why are We Here?

What sets man apart from all other living things? Sundry thoughts come to mind that might distinguish us from all other forms of life. Some might quibble and declare we are not so very different from a dandelion inasmuch as we share about eighty percent of it's DNA, or the very intelligent chimpanzee sharing ninety eight percent of our DNA. But, between either a twenty percent or two percent difference, there is an unbridgeable chasm separating dandelion, chimpanzees and humans. There is common DNA shared by most life forms but it's the other 20% or 2% that creates the vast chasm between a dandelion, a chimp or a human. We, who are modeled and made in the image of the Imago Dei, are as different as black night is from bright day without the tempering of a sunrise or a sunset, dawn or twilight. Just a pure blackness or a pure whiteness difference. We are very different from all other life forms including angels.

Art is one thing that separates us from other forms of life. We can all ponder as to why a dandelion or a chimpanzee cannot compose a concerto or paint the likeness of another; however, the chimp or the plant can never ponder on why we can do things and they cannot.

Laughing at a witticism or enjoying a good story is beyond all but man. I am sure angels can laugh, but there appears to be a dearth of information concerning this subject in Scripture. The angels and God certainly sing as we find in the Book of Job, Zephaniah and Revelation, however; God laughing is usually in the sense of derision at the foolishness of man. However, He rejoices over us as in Isaiah 62:5. Since we are made in His likeness, laughter surely began with Him. He will fill our mouths with laughter, Job 8:21 and will tell us when to laugh, Ecc. 3:4. He knows a cheerfull heart is good medicine Prov. 17:22. Likewise, to deny Jesus ever laughing is to deny His full humanity. He spoke of laughter in the Beatitudes, "Blessed are you who weep now, for you shall laugh." The humor in the idea of a camel going through the eye of a needle is comedic indeed in spite of it's other implications. The log in your eye is funny hyperbole. The joy before the angels of God over one sinner who repents tells me we are unique of all life on earth.

No one but man can wonder as to why we are here, where we are going and who put us here. No life form other than us or angels could ever contemplate the idea of heaven or hell. Since we see incompletely and imperfectly attests to the idea there must be something or someone complete and perfect. The Christian knows the Complete and Perfect is God, Yahweh, The Great I Am, The Alpha and Omega; this being the only true and permanent philosophy.

Reason is in fact an act of faith. If we rely strictly on reason, there is a danger of insanity. Philosophers are really no more than a form of religious zealots. Many philosophers and thinkers cannot factor in paradox. However, our entire existance is a paradox which can only be better understood by mystery. Ordinary man has always been a mystic, this mysticism being a kind of common sense. The common person knows about paradox and mystery intuitively. He accepts the paradox, therefore, understanding better; the illogical thinker tries to reconcile the paradox thus, understanding little.

God put the idea of eternity into our hearts Ecc 3:15 and if the truth be known, we know there is something wrong with us. Whether a savage or a suave salon, educated or uneducated, civilized or barbaric, all people sense they are broken. All have an innate knowledge of Another, a Mysterious One, Unknowable One; a pox on man's feeble attempts at explanations. Deep down we know we really don't know anything. The wisdom of Socrates was knowing this limitation. The babblers, the Sophists, the

Debaters and traveling Sages forever talking, deciding nothing testifies to the vacuousness of man's effort at understanding.

We desire truth but uncertainty remains. We really cannot prove much of anything. These deficiencies are evidence of our falleness. Just because we don't know or understand does not mean it is not true. By nature we know nothing about God, but what He reveals by nature, however; by faith which is dispensed by God we can know of His existance and nature. It is the heart that perceives God, not reason. Eternity exists and death ushers it in forcing us to make the decision of all time. Accept God on His terms or pay the unpayable note coming due.

The answer to the question of why we are here is to worship God and enjoy His creation which generates joy within us.

CHAPTER 6

Religion

Men are born unbalanced and some might even say they are insane, mad or diseased. The very word disease, dis-ease describes a state of not at ease. How easy it is for man to unintentionally invoke evil spirits since in some sense we are more familiar with these entities as a result of our original parents fall. There are enough strange religions in our world to fill a madhouse, hundreds of maniacal and often times crazy religions. However, the sometimes white hot hatred surrounding the church that Christ founded speaks volumes about it's truthfullness. So many people do not like the truth and would rather follow their manmade false belief systems. Christianity, however, has been proven by it's many miracles and hundreds of fulfilled prophecies. Other religions are shipwrecked upon the rocks of prophecy and miracles. Fallen man rage against their Creator; even kings it was said did this against His anointed, "Why do the heathen rage-the kings of the earth against His anointed?" Ps. 11:1-2.

Paradox is the key to truth and the ultimate paradox is Jesus Christ; fully human and fully God, the Hypostatic Union. There is no human way of understanding this paradox. Believing this requires humility to accept and therein lies the rub. Humility seems to go against the grain of humanity. Humility was found wanting in Lucifer the highest Cherubic order of angels and he, like me, opted instead for pride. Of course, this led to his downfall and all of mankind. Lucifer was not about to serve humans who he believed to be of a lower order than he and the other angels. The very word angel means to serve and minister to. According to the Book of Job, the angels were witnesses to the creation of everything including man. Lucifer was beautiful, powerful and incredibly intelligent therefore, he felt he and the other angels should not serve humans. Because of his disobedience and pride, God cast him and a third of the angels from heaven. Satan and his demonic hoard has been mankind's nemesis since. No other religion but Christianity has declared that man is born sinful; the other religions and philosophies are all telling us lies. Philosophers have made vices holy in contradistinction to Christians making virtues holy. Christianity is strange inasmuch as it bids man to view himself as wretched while at the same moment encourages him to be like God. In the end we are knowing and loving God above all else or we are left with the option of hating ourselves. If we know we are wretched, blind, filled with lust and pride and we refuse to be saved, then there is nothing left to say about that person. God has not hardened man's heart to unbelief; we are all born with hardened hearts. An enormous mystery is why would God chose some to open their eyes and soften their hearts to believe in Jesus, while others are left in their hardened states. Many theologians have thought upon this difficult subject, but scripture keeps leading them back to the hard truth. God always does the choosing. He is sovereign. There is a great chasm between knowing God and loving God.

Theology is always a belief whether one believes in it or not. Every person has a theology. They believe in something; themselves, their wealth, power, youthfullness, sports teams, friends, knowledge, etc. History tells us that unless it is centered in Judaic or Christian thought, people are prone to seek stranger sins trying to satiate their jaded senses. All men are inspired by religion be it good, or be it wicked, be it Yahweh or be it Baal. However, if God does not incline towards us; there is no other path open to us. We are left with absolute hopelessness. We are really only joyful when we surrender our stubborn will. A true Christian is more joyful, virtuous, lovable and reasonable in surrender. True conversion lies in self annihilation before a Holy God whom we so easily slander. A mediator is needed to deflect and absorb God's righteous wrath against our vileness. This mediator, Jesus Christ needs to negotiate an unnegotiable transaction. Now, this is enormously astounding. No one but humans, not even the angels are given this remedy. The angels upon one sin are forever condemned without recourse; whereas man with a vile sin nature who sins continually is viewed kindly by his Redeemer. Bethlehem is without doubt the touchstone at which extremes meet: Hopelessness and salvation. Since Jesus was born, all mythologies and philosophies have melted away.

Philosophers know about God but not their wretchedness, whereas atheists know their own wretchedness without knowing God, both positions lead to despair. It is intriguing to speculate upon why atheists spend so much time and effort in trying to disprove God. Being an agnostic makes more sense, they simpley do not need to believe. It's almost as if they do not put much energy or thought into the idea of whether there is a God or not. The atheist by definition is forever denouncing a God lending credible evidence that he believes there must by a God. Innumerable philosophers and learned people down through the ages have expended an inordinate amount of time and discussion defending atheism. As William Shakespeare wrote in the play Hamlet, "the lady doth protest too much, me thinks" as atheists inveigh against God. If one were to ask me how much time throughout the day I think about the "Flat earth society" or their belief in a flat earth, my response would be none. No time anytime is spent thinking about this nonsense. But, the atheist has spent eons of time trying to disprove God's existance. In so many ways, philosophy is nothing more than one more religion. How refreshing to think that no philosophy just might be the one true philosophy.

The crux of the whole matter is the Cross. The verticle beam straining towards God as the horizontal arm reaches towards mankind. The best the Wheel of Life of the Buddhist can accomplish is an endless going round and round with the spokes always leading inward to oneself. A shuddering helpless situation.

As stated well by G K Chesterton "whatever may be the meaning of faith, it must always mean a certainty about something we cannot prove. There is a certain mystery of consciousness. Religion and our desire and need for contemplating the unknown in every way differentiates us humans from other animals; for a human being, unlike animals, prays and laughs. People who worship a higher good see nature, people and the heavens move and change with the seasons, even though we will experience turmoil, fear and ultimately death as all do. We are more aware there is something greater and better than us.

Praying and striving to walk in the Commandments leads us to gentleness and peacefullness and a dignity that cannot be cancelled by death. Without religion and faith to guide us we will be left to war and the state to guide us. The best of us are our martyrs who have fought and died attempting to preserve these freedoms. They prove that worship and prayer is inviolate. They exemplify gentleness and charity. The meek shall inherit the earth.

Jesus Christ is the center of all things with all things trending towards Him. If you know this Christ then you know the reason for everything: Christian faith, not blind faith is common sense, whereas heresy usually lacks this feature. The only lasting thing in a chaotic and ever changing world is the Church Universal built upon the Rock of Jesus Christ which has endured for the last two thousand years. This church is a soothing balm and at the same time highly irritating to the world.

The gates of hell will not prevail against this Citadel. Not mystical John or the brilliant Paul were given the keys to this Church, but cowardly Peter, a snob and a weak man who reminds me of myself. A chain is only as strong as its weakest link and this Church has flourished because of weak links. Beginning at an empty grave, this church went forth with God again walking in a garden. Immediately all the simple messengers and Apostles boldly began telling a story; a Good Story, a true story and one that had never been told before. No other religion or movement has ever told this story; the Good News; simply because this story is true. The fact that our ancient religion has survived virtually intact lends credence to it's Divine origins.

Jews are so fond of prophecies, but so hostile to their fullfillment. Enoch, Noah and others prefigured the Christ. Noah saw the height of man's wickedness and in his seed saved the world. When God called Abram from pagan lands afar, He was revealing the mysteries of the coming Messiah. Jacob on his deathbed while blessing his children was interrupted by his rapturous utterances "I await the Savior whom thou has promised, O Lord." This was 1700 years before Christ was born. Moses seeing what the idolatrous Egyptians could not see, worshipped Yahweh, the one and only true God, 1500 years before the birth of Jesus.

In time the Greeks, Romans and others went about setting up their false gods and goddesses attended by their mystical, magical, marvelous myths. However, there were always chosen men from Judea and Israel fortelling the coming of a Messiah. The Patriarchs lived very long lives enabling them to spend hundreds of years with their children relating stories of geneologies. They were not burdened down as we are today with science, philosophy, arts or their studies. They lived talking about their ancestors. We can I believe, fail to appreciate the enormity and profoundness of this simple life. We see that creation and the flood were in an oral narrative tradition connecting Shem to Lamech who saw Adam, seeing Jacob who saw Moses. Any person can do what Mohammed and others have claimed, and start their own religion; but these people performed no miracles, foretold no prophecies, as Mohammed himself was not foretold. Neither Mohammed nor Buddha claimed to be God, but Christ did. No man stands as Christ stands.

If a simple man wrote a book foretelling the time and the manner of a forthcoming Messiah, he should be hailed and marveled at for disclosing such a prophecy. But to have many dozens of men in succession over a period of four thousand years proclaiming a future Messiah is on many levels and factors of ten different. Even under threat of persecutions and deprivations they held steadfast. The prophecies lend the most weight to the claim of Jesus being the Messiah. There are over 1,200 prophecies in the Bible and over 85% having already been realized. All have been fulfilled concerning Jesus' first coming and just a few left detailing His second coming. No other religion has one prophesy declared or realized. Hundreds of thousands of uneducated people did what Plato could not do in his Republic; make a few highly chosen people believe. Christ's wonderful church has always been under attack as it has stood against a fallen nature and our carnal pleasures. We Christians are expected to praise every creed save our own. As we argue on our own behalf we are labeled extremists or fundamentalist. So be it. Our apologia stands as others fall and are pierced by unsolvable riddles.

All manner of governments and religions that man has conjured has been man-centric. Of course this is so natural requiring little effort on our part. We like to view ourselves as central to the play and indeed we are to a degree, but with a few very important redeeming caveats. God is actually the center of all things and demands all praise, honor and glory. As important as we believe we are, and we are important, our allegiance and praise should be directed to our Creator; the God of all things. This is where we mess up. Like Lucifer, due to pride, we will not submit but want to be our own gods. The truth is we make terrible gods which is attested to by our dysfunctional world and our shattered lives. We need a helper, a friend, a redeemer to save us from ourselves and certain destruction and this has been provided us in the person of Jesus Christ.

All the important "isms" such as Communism, Socialism, Fascism, Stateism, Monarchism, Buddhism, Shintoism, Islamism, Animism, Judaism, Hinduism, Confucianism, Pantheism, New Ageism, Atheism and Nihilism all encourage man to improve himself by self effort. Most believe the problem lies outside ourselves and the solution lies within us. Through our own earnestness we can approach Nirvana, a better perfection. Human nature and history have been very clear about this misperception; it hasn't worked out so well for mankind.

Only Christianity has the answer as it pushes back against this relentless lemming like march to madness. Christianity diagnosis the problem as being internal with the only corrective being external.

We must look up towards God first. Being then, defined by Him, are we allowed to look inward at ourselves. At this time we can more correctly define ourselves, allowing us to then look outward presenting ourselves to the world a changed person. Man is an innate sinner, he can never help himself, he needs an external Friend to guide him. It is impossible for us to be good enough by our own efforts to win Paradise. Only Jesus the Christ has paid the price for entrance into the presence of God.

It was not that God was lonely and He needed to create us to make His joy complete. We are not the reason for the universe. God was and is always perfect in His companionship and love for His son Jesus Christ and the Holy Spirit. Each with the same essence but with different overlapping roles to perform in creation and history. God created not because of a lack of something, but out of an abundance of love. God is love. God the Father is the author of grace and love. Jesus Christ the Son is the provider and the Holy Spirit is the applicator of the love and grace. If allowed, God will pilot us to His celestial shore.

CHAPTER 7

---ww---

Early Man. Early Fall

After their sin and disobedience against an Omnipotent Creator, it seemed good to God to create a division separating one group of people from all other like minded heathens and pagans. He set the Semitic Hebrews, the future Jews apart from all other peoples. This was necessary for purifying and defining a group of people from whom a Messiah might appear. These people were the first to receive laws, dispensed by God and recorded by Moses. This was a thousand years before any semblance of laws appeared in the ancient Greek culture. No laws were recorded by Homer in his epic stories of the Odyssey or Iliad are mentioned for example.

The very ancient Abram the future Abraham was separated from his pagan ancestors and used by God for His Grand Plan. Now a true paradox appears. There obviously was history before history; we just don't know what it contained since it was not recorded and written down. We know very little about pre history people precisely because they were pre history. However, there are traces of humanity before there were human stories. Human civilization is older than human records with art predating languages.

Rationalists often indulge in unreason and rampant speculations in an attempt to tell the story of prehistory early man. Now our vaunted anthropologist and the vast genera of scientists studying antiquity read with sometimes too vivid of an imagination deciphering an incredible amount of information pertaining to a man in a pictograph. Maybe this prehistory man, woman, or child might have been just taking pleasure in the joy of drawing what was around them in their world. We now have "experts" thousands of years removed from the events taking it upon themselves ascribing all manner of religions, the afterlife, and other fantasies to these early people. The hapless prehistory person may have just been drawing for the sheer joy of it; much as would a Van Gogh or Rembrandt might, or a child just dwaddling. Scientists have constructed a fantastical rendering of ancient man based on little more than artful pictures and missing links in paleontology.

We know so very little but this seldom prevents our imaginations from running wild. We conjure up a language or no language, a cave man dragging a woman around by her hair, societies invoking evil spirits or good spirits, strong or weak chieftains and all manner of condescending trivia. Maybe J.R. Tolkien was onto something in his fabulous tale of the Hobbitts, but we know this to be fantasy. I believe scientists and others have also written a fantasy, but one of which they believe. At the expense of common sense, they have constructed an entire family tree with us of course perched at the top. Poor prehistory man is at a great disadvantage in this scheme. But the fact of the matter is this; the dawn of written history already reveals a humanity civilized. Egypt, Babylonia, and others lend strong credence to the argument these people were more advanced than the popular rendering of the savage cave man.

It takes little learning in the making of a healthy mind. Too much learning in a narrow sense might lead to unhealthy speculations and conclusions. An open mind is really not a great virtue, it is designed to come to a conclusion. Not to do so leads to foolishness. We parse the imperfections of our ancestors from a position of comfort which through time they labored to provide.

Ancient people I surmise were very much just like us. Hard working, family or tribe oriented, defenders of life, religious, dreamers and thinkers. What utter condescension on our part believing we are the "cats meow". At times we move as popinjays extolling our merits while we pound "primitive" people. Man has and will always remain man with all his warts and glory.

CHAPTER 8

Life, Children, Sacrifice and Diversions

"To be or not to be" might be the question, but the answer is a resounding Be! The affirmations, the celebrations of life and the wonderment itself should always be what we desire. In contradistinction to encouraging life is the taking of a life either through murderous passions or if sanctioned by the state resulting in executions. The taking of life should always be a sober and grievous deed. However, there is a type of murder so diabolical even the Romans shunned the practice. This empire which at time was so violent and capable of much evil, did not traffic in child sacrifices. The Baals and Molech demonic gods were insatiable in their lust and thirst for child sacrifice, which appears only the "higher" civilizations practiced. The less developed and more "savage" peoples did not participate in this barbarism with their attendant and organized rituals. No indigenous people of the far North or Aborigines of Australia indulged themselves in child sacrifice or cannibalism.

The Romans when not desiring a child to raise would allow the child to be born and then placed the unwanted baby by the side of the road or byway letting the Fates deal with it. Often passerbys, usually Christians, would rescue the baby taking it home to raise. Much like baby Moses who was put aside, they had a chance of rescue. This is one example of early Christians standing out and being viewed differently by the pagan Romans. Who would rescue such a child unless to raise as a slave? Christians should always be seen as peculiar and in the world, but not of the world.

Even the advanced Aztecs and Myans usually sacrificed older children and young adults, not infants; however, not our current "sophisticated" society. We sacrifice the most innocent and helpless of all while they are encosed in the safety of the maternal womb. This man-made right to infanticide has now been enshrined in our highest laws. Millions upon tens of millions of innocents sacrificed upon the altar of convenience to our everlasting shame. Paraphrasing saintly Mother Teresa "a society that so easily kills it's innocent children in this manner is capable of any evil". How correct she was. C.S. Lewis points out we are souls, not just bodies. We are souls with bodies. When babies are aborted, their souls will live on even as their bodies are destroyed. This sober realization should stop us in our tracks as we march forward slaughtering more little bodies. There will be a day of reckoning for those approving. The apostle Paul speaks to this in Romans 1:32 "and although they know the ordinance of God, that those who practice such things are worthy of death; they not only do the same, but also give hearty approval to these who practice them".

We are filled with natural error that can only be corrected by grace. The only two principles of truth afforded us are our senses and our reason both of which can deceive since both traffic in lies and deception. Barbarism and civilization have always existed side by side. Just because a majority believes one way does not necessarily make their opinions clearer or correct. The simplest of people often have the most subtle of ideas which at times may appear ignorant to us; but like a child they may know more than what they can explain. As the Greek sage Heraclitus stated "Man is most nearly himself when he achieves the seriousness of a child at play."

This confusion about life is a clear manifestation of mankinds falleness. Our thinking is rife with error. When the world wobbles and goes astray, it lends strong evidence that the Christian Church is correct. The Church Universal is justified not because her children do not sin, but because they do. We often despise religion being afraid it could be true. Usually however, a civilization that has a little more religion influencing it probably has more reason about it. Of course theocracies must always be shunned. People without faith cannot really know true goodness or true justice.

All our dignity consists in thought; we should think well which will then lead us to a basic virtuous morality. As Vicktor Frankle the survivor of concentration camps said "There are only two kinds of people, the decent and the indecent." We cannot reach sanity until we appreciate sanctity. Men can and do change. The most cruel and depraved concentration camp guards in Nazi Germany and Imperial Japan in WW2 at times were seen to morph into decent people. No one is purely indecent or decent and each group always have some of each. There is always hope of redemption for all of us as Christ taught, we should forgive seventy times seventy. The only one who can help us to forgive is God.

Between heaven and hell a most amazing thing exists, life a most fragile thing. The wisest thought we can have concerning the subject of life is "In the beginning" some unthinkable Power did some unthinkable thing. We are incapable of understanding and it is not necessary that we do. Something that is incomprehensible does not mean it cannot exist. Science is incapable of solving the riddle of life so our default position is to let the philosophers deal with it. The problem being that all of philosophy is probably not worth an hour's effort of study. Mumbo jumbo inanities veneered with a thick layer of vanity. Anyone who cannot see the vanity of this world are themselves vain. Since we are unable to understand life, cure death, deal with our own wretchedness or our deep ignorance of all things of import, we choose to not think too deeply upon these matters.

We need diversions to keep us occupied and happy. Diversions narcotizes our wretchedness and lulls us gently to our deaths. Remove our diversions, our trinkets and leave us alone with our thoughts is frightening to most. Give them anything for a diversion even pain, but don't leave them alone with their own thoughts. It can drive one mad. Only youth with it's diversions and inanities may be given a pass, but even they can see the nullity of their existance when removing their eyes from the trinkets.

Exploring deeper this tension of now and the future, great stress is placed on the individual in yearning for more, better, a different image of self. As mentioned, diversions and trinkets can only narcotize but there may be a better way.

We seem to be in such a hurry; a hurry to arrive at some future destination. Improving ourselves, pushing ourselves, developing plans and timetables to arrive at a future better us. But what might we be missing by taking this journey? I might be better off if I stopped trying to get somewhere else, be someone else and cease conjuring a "better" reality. What if I were able to live life in the awe of now and be present in all the now moments. On my journey forward upon arriving, I will find its just another now. If now is all we really have, can we bare that existance? However, if we can truly endure the now and fully embrace it then we may start to see time differently; more of a verticle experience rather than a horizontal one. We can then drop down into a deeper verticle infinity and rest in that moment. All my true wants will be brightly illumined letting me see my true want is to be right where I am at the moment.

I want this moment to be everything, whatever it is, I am in awe actually that I get to be here at all. Stop striving to be somewhere else and strive to be here in the now. This might be a singular achievement in our lifetime. Society encourages us to always strive - might it just be better to strive to be in the now as my life happens? A sought after destination should be here now. The journey to where we are is the most remarkable journey we will ever embark upon.

Now, of course, it is natural for children to eventually mature into adults. However, in Western civilization and especially in America where it was birthed, teenagers appeared. This artificial delay of a child becoming an adult in society was created out of fear and guilt following WW2. A desire to protect and ease our children's burdens created a nether world where a child could forever develop a Peter Pan personality allowing others to care for their responsibilities. We now have perpetual boys who shave like men but still act with a mindset of a boy, not taking responsibility surrounding themselves with like-minded men-boys who play games.

Since a vacuum existed, it was filled by women who were thrust into the role of mother and father. Out of this milieu of nonsense, society suffered. There is really nothing positive to say about this experiment. Madison Avenue has grown wealthy in hawking this product. These teenagers have been given license to remain insipid, and condescending toward adults all the while remaining vain and shallow. This societal experiment which is supported by many psychologists has been a failure leading to many unhealthy activities. It's almost as if we are in a big experiment with us as the guinea pigs. I believe the results are portending poorly and it might be to late to correct the damaging results. We are being disconnected from each other, not more connected. There is an overwhelming amount of information which we cannot properly process. Facebook friends but few real friends. The old ways are frowned upon. Digital money, crypto currency at the expense of real money. On and on this slow trainwreck unfolds before us as we continue to navigate these interesting times.

Here I am not speaking against the idea of childhood or children per se. The hatred of the idea of childhood is certainly demonic. Witches using black magic to lure children to an oven to burn them or even the idea of child martyrs in the Middle Ages is demonstrably evil. Satans minions have always encouraged the destruction of life. The most vulnerable are always the infants and children. From the time of the Hebrew prophets to the present requires an enormous effort to protect children. So in one sense, it makes some sense to prolong childhood as long as possible thus allowing for parental protections, keeping evil at bay.

Leaving for now the discussion concerning children, I will explore the unique institution of family. But it is comforting to know the old trinity or the human trinity is the father, mother, and child mirrowing the structure of the Divine Trinity. It will always be this way to the chagrin of "modern thought".

CHAPTER 9

——⌇——

Family

We step into a fairy tale like adventure when we are born. Startling and wonderful at times as we step into a family; hardly believable, but always fantastic, colorful and even romantic. If one is graced to be inserted into a family with wonderful parents and exciting siblings, then they are approaching rarely attained nirvana. The ultimate human institution is the sacred family unit which, of course, is under continuous attack. To be enconsed in a family is a good thing even as the howls of all enemies rain down upon it. There is a sense of safety and comfort as if a raging blizzard was just outside the strong walls. Of course the skeptics suggest that the family is not always congenial and of course they are correct. But the family is good and wholesome, however, there can be discord and divisions. It is clear that if a family can function and navigate through turmoil in spite of their differences, is proof enough that they can function in the larger society. To revolt against family is to revolt against an ordered nature. Stepping into our family at birth, the challenge facing all humankind is how to get along with these people. This is all part of God's marvelous plan. Each day a new chapter unfolds before us as we, with abated breath, await the next.

The home is the only place of freedom and liberty. The ordinary man wants ordinary things; a home that fits, the freedom to fall in love, marry, have children and become a grandparent. Just to be an ordinary hero to the family around him is something to strive for. However, big business and big government conspire against the family. The truth is obvious, this ordinary parent with his ordinary family is the bedrock foundation holding all society together; it fails, society fails.

Preserving the family requires us to live simpler lives. We need to be more content with less. Being content is to be free. Dispair does not happen because of suffering but in being discontented with not having more. When good things in a society no longer pleases, that society starts to decline - ergo America. A well lived simple life is meaningful and beautiful for all time. As stated earlier, we all crave simplicity not complexity. Our society is now designed to keep us agitated, wanting more, lustful of what others might have. Our news sources, our entertainments, our literature, everything is coming against the truth. Only the family allows us freedom. We have always been prone to wander and losing our way, but we always remembered our address and eventually found our way back home. Today we are in great peril as we struggle to remember where we live; almost like one with dementia.

The great ongoing experiment of social media keeps us continually connected and agitated by cascades of never ending information and enticements. This does not well augur for the health of the family. I will not spend anymore time in discussing the wonderments or the devilishness of the internet. We probably all have an innate sense we have made a faustian bargain with the devil at some level. Man has always proved he can take something good and by unintended alchemy turn it to bad.

I longingly vote for a simple life without too much puffery and an air of peasantry about it, and with my own little property, with spouse and family about. This is the idealized bedrock of a civilized society. Big business and big government is poison to the sacred family, the human trinity of Mother, Father and child. Please leave me alone as I pursue my life as you pursue yours.

CHAPTER 10

—⁓—

Friends

Mighty mountain rising from the plain
is a person, moniker for a name.
Some linger a lengthy bit
others gone in a hop and a skip.
Each serves a special need,
stanchion, a piller a wavering reed.
This one I would die for but now can get lost,
my needs so fickle and comes at great cost.
I am fair weathered and so are they,
many file through but few will stay.
You must know me inside and out
my shine, my stain, my sin and my pout.
If you don't turn and depart from me,
if you don't faint from all that you see
then I might gaze and discern upon you
judging you harshly to see what you do.
If you are still standing with love in your heart,
a friendship beginning a glorious start.
You seem to know me all pretense being gone
I'am just myself for this I have longed.
Knowing and being known no averting of eye,
you love me all my warts and my sty.
This happens rarely a few times in one's life,
all others are fillers where drama is rife.

This one I know and they me,

speaking or silence whatever we please.

Near or distant matters little to us,

boundries, spatials are just a mere fuss.

Time goes by and the relationship grows,

souls reverberating, resonating love shows.

This good gift of God a foretaste of glory,

no shielding or veil just my blemished story.

I am as you see me needy and weak

these saints these friends the ones that I seek.

"Each friend represents a world in us, a world possibly not born until they arrive," beautifully written by French essayist Anais Nin in 1937. The arrival of a new friend awakens in us our true identity.

The very idea of friendship is complicated. First and foremost, having a friend is a good thing as all good things are from God. There is no other relationship as grand as a good friend. Our standing with God should be paramount followed by our best friend, our beloved spouse. However, there are wonderful moments in our lives when a person comes along beside us joining in our walk. There is almost something mystical about this chemistry of kindred spirits. Through magical alchemy the drab becomes the gold. Oh, how easy it is to talk with this person, to want what they want, to hurt when they hurt, dream together, fly away together, be close, be far, talk, don't talk, knowing at some deeper level your souls reverberate with love. We were made for this. The comfort and sense of feeling safe, where you need not weigh your thoughts or measure out your words but knowing your friend will take all, the chaff and the grain and sift it well. They will keep whats worth keeping and with a kind breath blow the rest away.

I have come to realize over a long life that these relationships come and go away; few endure the long journey together. What was so important and urgent in the moment, a thing that was always going to be there, trails off into a has been friend, demoted to an acquaintance. The meaning, the mettle, the binding ingredients all have waned. In a way it is as if two ships have passed in the night; each quietly sailing for it's own harbor. But while they were passing the world was our oyster. We were stalwart, we were fearless, we were hopeful. We understood each other completely. As often happens, life gets in the way, demanding what cannot be provided and the relationship is pulled asunder. These people filled my needs at the time as I filled theirs.

A truly lasting old tenured friendship is a rare jewel. It takes nurturing, humility and an awareness of what one has in this jewel. Often the relationship flounders as if striking an unseen obstacle. It might be nothing more than a silly argument that puts distance betwcen people. Hopefully as these relationships change we can learn from the failure. This situation happened with my best friend when our friendship unraveled over a disagreement and the man I so looked up to and so admired who I believed would be my old man dear friend came to a sudden end. I grieved over this loss for many years finally realizing that God had orchestrated this dissolvement for my own good and growth. It seemed as if I had put too much time and attention into this relationship at the expense of others. In essence, God ended the friendship allowing me to mature and be stretched in ways unknown to me at the time. The feeling is that friendships are not static but ever evolving. New ones come as old ones wanes however, a few will remain to our last breath.

Bobby Jones is a dear friend I have known for over 68 years and another, Karen MacFarland for over 46 years. Many of my friends have passed away leaving me with just a few cherished ones. I have however, developed new friends in my older age and they bring me great pleasure. Having a drink with Glen Gravatt and enjoying a fine cigar in the evening is priceless. We two have solved many of the worlds problems using just these two simple ingredients.

It's rare that one can know another a 100 percent, but that should be our goal. No secrets, no minimizing, but sought after total transparency. No 99 percent known which is not being known at all but the rare coveted 100 percent which leaves the devil no room to play. Of course, this is difficult and only a few will ever attain this level of intimacy. Proverbs 18:24 declares "But there is a friend who sticks closer than a brother." None is an island to themselves as we all know; we were made for community with others and we long for a few friends. The Roman sage Seneca said it well, "The comfort of having a friend may be taken away, but not that of having had one".

Friends just make our lives more complete. As they come and go, part of them and their unique stories intermingle with ours resulting in a more interesting tapestry.

CHAPTER 11

Hell

The afterlife is real whether you believe it or not. There are only two possible destinations which beckons us, heaven or hell. I will speak of hell first. This is a real place spoken of in the Holy Bible. As a matter of fact, Jesus Himself spoke about hell and it's dangers more than He spoke of heaven. Trying to avoid the topic, man has demoted hell to a myth and the devil is now a cartoonish character with horns and cloven feet. However, you trifle with hell at your own risk. It is a terrible place with Lazarus entreating Abraham for any kind of relief. The Bible describes hell as a place of no light as all light emanates from God who is Light. You will not be hanging out with your buddies as friendships are good and from God. You in fact, will be repulsed away from people. You will forever be falling and your main sin that caused you to be in hell will forever be before you - "your worm never dies". You will forever become more evil, vile and deranged. Your punishment will be for eternity as a price for rejecting God's gracious offer of salvation. There is no annihilation theology in hell. I will now let poetry, which I have penned discuss this subject which staggers the mind.

> Me lying in repose a dreamy sleep
> now thrust violently down into the deep.
>
> Arriving, I to iron gates of Hell
> near fainting, swooning can I prevail?

Why I to this hellish portal sent
believing my life a saint bespent?

Racked with fear a quaking uncertain
gates open slowly like scrofulous curtain.

Propelled through gate by unseen force
my feet set on dim lit course.

Delorous souls neath marshy Styx descend
tristful moment gives pause in this filthy fen.

Dangerous sable mire,
tormented souls weary, tire.

Gasping, besmirch they do all reek
terror, grasping relief they so seek.

Lady Wisdom she watches in repose blissful
agonies of judgement on wanton the wistful.

Heaping blasphemes and a curse
on this wise Ladies open purse.

"Take freely from me to thee
you descending neath lurid sea."

You imbelic creatures your ignorance vast,
sins heaping up from now to past.

Avarice and greed your tresses shorn
gold you sought fails to adorn.

In your groanings your eternal scruffle
searching in vain for the tasty truffle.

Cardinals, Popes, others of their ilk
ill gotten lucre, cathedrals were built.

Plutus calling forth Papé Satan below,
as the damned receive a thunderous blow.

Be wary of accursed wolf with bloated lip,
standing on rotten parchment you just might slip.

Philosophers, Sages round about go,
rhetoric, arguments shrill and bold.

They are foolish and pseudo-wise,
Omnipotent One they so despised.

Ever so close to Paradise
eschewing Pascal never threw dice.

Betting to avoid the craggy dell
plunge themselves to a fiery hell.

Each will find their eternal tomb
destined they from mother's womb.

From all eternity re-echoes refrain
changing of choir they dare not deign.

Perfection they can never attain
seeking succor in pleasure and pain.

Teach me still I wish thee
comfort my shuddering soul for me.

Their souls Hell will forever envenom
the sweetness of Heaven never for them.

Into the gullet rapacious
the wormwood flowing insatious.

As honey drops like dew
shrewd Screwtape ensnares his few.

Illicit lovers embrace, entwining
lips kiss forever now dying.

Tensioned agonies on sable wings
tormented lover croons and sings.

This place of darkness mute of light
faint of heart dies of fright.

A place is this where nothing shines
even late twilight countenance pines.

No vermillion hue or shimmering blue
deathly darkness covers, subdues.

Autumnal leaves fall from stately tree
falling like stars, Adams seed.

Devils with their eyes of gleed,
poke and probe, souls they bleed.

Lady of Virture, Lady of Lore
She standing athwart Hells open door.

Entreating she pleads do repent
if not you eternity here bespent.

Heretics entombed in sepulchers vile
lamenting, tortured all the while.

Portal of future closes on wholly dead
choaking miasma covers all with dread.

Every sin that wins hate in Heaven
coveting and pride spreads it's leaven.

These felons of the hellish fire
belch blasphemes of their Father, the Liar.

Minataur the fictious half man half beast
Satans creature lashes all great and least.

Descending farther into the neather Hell
forbidden here to rest a spell.

Wrath insane hands to head
dreadful souls moan in dread.

Thousands emerging from the moat
fall under salvo of arrows smote.

The boiled in the reddish fire
no hallelujah sang this hellish choir.

Tyrants who made so much war
their punishment measured by meter, score.

Harpies laughing their hideous laugh
Wolfhounds tear limbs like splintered staff.

Being tender when being stroked
but fierce when being provoked.

The burning sand set on fire
falling embers of heat it's desire.

Dancing feavered Shades shaking the gleeds,
removing these embers their primary need.

Arrogance, distain a blinding rage
many kings dance in a fiery cage.

Crying, begging for extinguishment,
no rain from Heaven ever sent

The monster with its pointed tail
infects the world with untold travail.

Unclean image of woeful deceit
lashes tail, stomps it's feet.

Quivering tail sweeping void
forked tongue it's aneroid.

Scorpions sting like driving daggers
all it touches moans and staggers.

But I did see that dragon Belzelbub
He with stinking blood did rub

on his hideous face and arms
absent of every good and charm

With three heads each a face
faint smirk you discern and trace.

Crunching a sinner in each mouth
bones protruding from it's snout.

The beautiful Lucifer when he fell
now the monster of the lowest Hell.

Every person of their kind
Judas, Hitler their ilk will find

Falling to the lowest pit
as the Dragon rends and spits.

All the ones innumerable Saint slayers
their sins stacked layer by layer.

They deflowered the Imago Dei
at this moment they will pay.

Munching and crunching bones splitting wide
their worm their temptation never dies.

Coughing a plea for annihilation
no hope for that in this situation

In my dream my soul was vexed
I had no desire to see whats next.

Closing my eyes against swirling haints
I struggle to remember I am a Saint.

Hell no terror for me
in my error

No murmur nor tortuous moan
will my body or soul own.

The transaction by Messiah was made
rising from tomb where He laid.

Opening of eyes
I long for beautious sky

Beads of water bejewel my brow
spending time in Hell just an hour

Some would rather reign in Hell
than serve in Heaven doing well.

Hell where is your victory?
Satan no more cunning or trickery.

Death where is your sting?
While Heaven ever rings and sings.

Beloved Son to Hell he went
assuring me I will never be sent.

CHAPTER 12

Heaven

As Hell is horrifying to contemplate, Heaven is many factors of ten better to dwell upon. The very idea of a heaven lends considerable support to the concept of a Transcendent God. At a deep level all men know this place is beyond the capabilities of mankind to construct. So once again the hapless atheist is left to explain where the hope of Heaven originated. God revealed snippets of this majestic unimaginable place in His revealed word in the Bible such as Revelation. The Son of Thunder was so overwhelmed at the vision given him that he staggered and fainted at the sight. As the Psalmist spoke gloriously of Heaven, this is the medium I will use in a feeble attempt at my depiction of Paradise.

Closing of eyes First Heaven went through
Second Heaven vast its entirely true.

Third Heaven is where I will reside
Trinity and Paul ever by my side.

Constantine eagle bird, of God
was used of God given gracious nod.

One nature to exist in Christ not more
one plus three is one the score.

This little planet I dance upon
one day will be swept, purged and gone.

Diverse voices sweet melody make
shimmering Shades in Heaven partake.

Five daughters of Zelophehad each a queen
passes through this heavenly scene.

Blindly staggering men below
in need of Life Saver this we know.

To God, to Jews one death was pleasing,
Christ on cross man's pain was easing.

Human creature his nobility falling
thrust spear into God's Darling.

Man with limitations has no power
driven from Garden his mood was sour.

Goodness Divine who imprints the world
deemed it gracious restoring man his Pearl.

God bounteous himself to give
stopping man's hellish skid.

All other modes being insufficient,
God Incarnate His timing propitious.

In the Third Heaven where I stand
I behold first the high Seraphim.

Some in front those behind
sing sweet hosannas, sweet divine.

I beheld the Spirit the Holy One
Restrainer of evil shining as Holy Sun.

Lamentations will follow us all our days
as we rebelled and went astray.

But this Holy Light which was given
throughout our souls with Love was riven.

Mirrors, as thrones they be
judicious God shines on me.

As a fine ruby smitten by sun
efflugence through me like river runs.

No repentance here we shine
near to Father Abba Divine.

Here beside me scintillating
journey over no more waiting.

Now inside me there is rest
even Holy Rahab passed her test.

Faithful unto Joshua taking her stand
allowing he and Caleb to enter God's holy land.

Because of Christs triumph she was taken up
forever to recline with her Savior sup.

The Primal and Unutterable Power
Beneficent on all does shower.

Lucent in Himself as a thousand blazing suns,
gazing on this One our soul and spirit undone.

And if our fantasies to lowly are
conjuring only takes us so far.

Give thanks to the Sun of Angels
only Son who untangled the tangles.

Within the court of Heaven many jewels found
each pouring forth a joyous sound.

I see in the radiance of His grace
a gem for me singing in place.

I am a lamb of his Holy flock
my Redeemer, Tower, my Gate, my Rock.

I see Peter, the poor widows mite
both holy precious in God's sight.

Holy choir sings and chants
Spirits and Angels join in dance.

So loved of God the barefooted beggars
move with grace with peaceful Quakers.

When I first feel the frost of death
for me this be my place of rest.

The Divine nature persons three
for all time human, Divine will be.

The One, the Two, the Three ever lives
coruscant Love all Three gives.

That which can die and dieth not,
God constructs the Gordian knot.

Love lucent flows from glorious Three
even as One died on the tree.

Stamping their signet on Holy Wax
paying for sins hellish tax.

Lovely Virtue can break this seal
allowing many to hear Heavens peal.

Wise King Solomon in his greatness did learn
fear God vain man and it's Heaven you earn.

For very low among the fool is he
who supposes he is wise unto God will be.

Sabellius, Pelagus, Arius for sure
not here resides but with common cur.

For us our glorious flesh reassumed
sanctified our spirits will forever bloom.

My vision of Heaven of course must increase
as my limitations and assumptions forever decrease.

The Holy Spirit sparkling like fire
directs my heart to Him my desire.

Taking His cross and following Christ
I wooed by Spirit to Paradise.

God the missionary sent his Son
proceeded by Spirit my heart was won.

God is a father ever before ruler
each Saint a gem set by Master Jeweler

Unconditional love no shame concerning me
resting in Abrahams bosom paradise I see.

Released from bonds of a fallacious world
I here esteemed as a precious pearl.

Some come here by martyrdom
me by pastors preaching sum.

Sheepfold of sainted John be found
they are the ones Heaven bound.

As birds arising from the shore
they find themselves now at Heaven's door.

Rainbow tears of sainted mothers,
shed losing sons and brothers.

Son of Glory wipes the eyes
no one here will ever cry.

Illume with Thyself Divine
your beauty within me so sublime

The soldiery of Heaven whom I contemplate
sing hosannas to One their glorious fate.

I knew not the fishermen nor Paul
but here I see them one and all.

The pleasing aroma of these perpetual flowers
waft to the One with all the powers.

Oh gentle Love with a smile cloaking thee
let this smile forever clothe me.

Cascades of Love we sit under
Hallelujah voices peal like thunder.

In awe we bow in Holy worship
praising Him for His costly purchase.

No merit of mine ever brought me here
predestined from eternity with Love not fear.

Melting the frost of my heart so hoary
He who keeps the key to all glory.

He feeds me supper from His celestial table
all gather round as we are able.

Serving me with His scarred Holy hands
Heaven resounds with Angelic bands.

One in Himself remaining as before
One who ushered me through Heaven's door.

Like unto rubies that are set in gold
this Light of God forever glows

The saintly host as of a snow white rose
the Bride of Christ we all arose.

Bridegroom awaiting His spotless Bride
we the Church His everlasting pride.

He comes tenderly embracing our souls
His glory our joy the eternal goal.

Oh Light eternal sole comforter of my soul
worshipping Triune God my eternal goal.

Abba, Daddy I am now home
never again to wander or roam.

CHAPTER 13

———— ∾∾∾ ————

Government

Paraphrasing Plato who said "If you have no interest in the affairs of government, then you will be destined to be ruled by fools, or James Madison, an early American president stating "If men were angels, no government would be needed.

The concept of government is rather interesting. People it appears, have a need or desire to be led and guided by a smaller cadre of others. It seems this is a necessitity for mankind to flourish. If each were left to their own ways, anarchy would prevail. Tribalism would be the norm with small groups vying for resources and outright domination. Countering this constant agitation, people groups with common ancestry and territories naturally coalesced into larger groups, which then required a more centralized governing nexus, with more power concentrated in fewer people. Because of this necessity the seeds of much sorrow were unintentionally planted. Man has always had a propensity to take something good and make it ungood. We cannot resist the temptation to rule. As Lord Acton correctly stated "power corrupts, absolute power absolutely corrupts."

A benevolent government showering beneficence on it's citizens is an almost unrealized dream. Usually, however; it is the upper strata or caste of citizens that is smiled upon as the lesser strata struggles to survive. Nevertheless, at certain times in history a benevolent Monarchy has ruled, this especially being seen in Europe. A sovereign keeping a kind watch over his serfdom ruled in a more tender way. A pleasant despot is a rarity, a kind tyrant an oxymoron. The privileged in power have always lorded over it's underlings.

Now there are examples of governments so abominable they leap from the pages of history. The licentious Roman emperors such as Caligula, the atrocities of the Assyrians, Babylonians and others come to mind. Of course, there have always been individuals holding great power who viciously wielded their might such as Genghis Khan, certain Tzars of Russia and the various kingdoms of China and other parts of Asia which were led by violent men.

Institutions holding great power such as the Catholic Church were responsible for much misery and suffering in the persecutions during the Inquisitions. Theocracies always results in despotic governments. When organized religion becomes intimate with a government, an unhealthy spawn is produced. The church tends to become the whore of the government. The government will always change the church as evidenced by the Reich Church of Nazi Germany remaining silent or even becoming an apologist for the machinations of the Nazis. Eighty per cent of the mainline Protestant denominations backed the Nazi regime, either because of fear or often due to the proffered promise of power. Even at times, the Catholic Church was suspect in its silence concerning the holocaust as evidenced by the apologies of Pope Pius the 4th. Standing against this diabolism was the Confessing Church of Germany championed and led by the martyred and heroic Dietrich Bonhoffer. Bonhoffer, the brilliant German theologian was bold in his denunciation of Nazism. He certainly could have remained safe in the United States where he was studying, however, against advice, he returned to Germany to rail against Hitler. He wrote and taught in his outlawed seminaries and actively worked against the evil state. The Reich church took the less dangerous common path and parroted the talking points of Hitlerism. Finally imprisoned in the very last days of the Third Reich, Hitler had him hung from gallows. Later, Hitler committed suicide; a pox upon the cowardly Evangelical and Catholic churches of Germany. We need and must always stand on the side of goodness and truth no matter the cost.

A current example of church and state commingling is in Muslim countries. The Islamic religion is many times intrinsically linked with the government forming a Theocracy. This became the pattern after Mohammed was forced from Mecca and fled to Medina where he set up operations. This was necessary because the Christians and Jews in Mecca grew tired of his proselytizing. They demanded he provide a miracle or a prophecy to substantiate his claims of which he could provide neither. He became much more aggressive when he fled to Medina where the remaining three fourths of the Quran was written. The first third written while in Mecca, is much more benevolent than the last three fourths written in Medina. The religion rapidly spread by means of intimidation and warfare. The Middle East was conquered with Christians and Jews being overwhelmed. Entire populations and communities which had been present for over a thousand years were suddenly gone. This militant Muslim contagion moved into Europe until Charles Martel halted the advance at the Battle of Tours in 754. The Christian Crusades, all twelve of them over a period of one hundred years were in response to the continuous Islamic invasions. No one ever becomes a Christian by threat of sword but this has been the modus operandi for the conversion to Islam. The very word Islam means submission. There is a great difference between Allah (the appropriated Moon god of India,) and Yahweh the Great "I am who I am."

Man has always had it in his heart to enslave his fellow man, to control another. This is a defect in our thinking. The Egyptians thought it advantageous to enslave the Israelites as did the Assyrians and Babylonians. Even when given the chance, the Jews enslaved. Within the populations of the Roman Empire there were an estimated sixty million slaves. Slavery has been profitable for all countries of the world which relies heavily on the labors of indentured others for the easement of the life of the master. This abomination was practiced by Native Americans long before America was settled by White Europeans. Slavery was also common on the continent of Africa and in fact was practiced throughout the world. The worlds economy was indeed powered by slavery. In rebuttal to Cancel-Culture and Revisionist history, America was not founded for the propagation of this vile practice. This entire nonsense will be dealt with in another chapter but suffice it to say, this is a play right out of the Communist Manifesto.

William Wilberforce and William Pitt, the Prime Minister of England; two white Christian men with aid from the Clampham Society of 1840 England were finally able to legally outlaw slavery in the British Empire. The United States fighting a civil war resulting in over six hundred thousand deaths quickly followed the lead of England with France not far behind. Of note, these were all Christian nations in the forefront of ending slavery. However, the last country to outlaw slavery was the Muslim nation of Muritania in 1981. The very fact it is now outlawed worldwide does not mean it still does not exist. Human trafficking and the sex trade both being forms of slavery are flourishing with at least 20-30 million people indentured.

Many Islamic cultures still enslave people such as in Somalia and the Sudan just as the Communist Chinese does it's Muslim population of Uighygurs.

All forms of despotism are despicable and as often stated; right without might is impotent, might without right tyrannical. The individual is still often insignificant before the State and just being able to survive multiple defeats is a triumph.

The system that has lifted more people from poverty to the middle class and beyond is Capitalism. Of course, it is an imperfect model but still the best to date. When Capitalism is wed with a Constitutional Republicanism it is the best form of government man has been able to create. It far surpasses and outpaces all other forms of government in enabling people to dream and strive. Our Founding Fathers with much study and even as imperfect men were able with Divine guidance to devise this system which has benefited untold millions in the past 250 years.

This form of Constitutional Republicanism has in some form been practiced by the oldest continually surviving nation in the world. The small nation state of San Marino has existed since it's founding in 351 A.D. and for over 1700 years this Christian nation has tended to it's own affairs leaving the world to mind it's own. The citizens are kind and friendly to each other and are governed by two co-equal Prime Ministers who hold terms of only six months so no one person can amass great power or wealth by corruption. It would bode well for all nations to heed this example of government. This country is also a great proponent of Capitalism.

Great minds such as Edmund Burke, John Locke, Charles Montesquieu, Thomas Jefferson, John Adams, James Madison and many others were responsible for this revelatory idea of a Constitutional Republic type of government. It had never been thought of or tried before. However, there are many rubs in this system. One such rub requires a civilized society, people being nice to each other. Another challenge requires an educated populace. These duties required of a population over a period of time can become burdensome and tiring. It requires great effort to remain a free people. The irony is that the more civilized a society becomes, the greater the chance of despotism developing. Democracy breaks down as civilization becomes more complex which requires more effort by all citizens. Tyranny many times is a result of a tired democracy. We become too worn out to defend liberty; let someone else do it. "Freedom is never more than one generation from extinction. It must be fought for, protected and handed to our children to do the same, or one day we will spend our sunset years telling our children what it was once like in the United States where men were free." Ronald Reagan.

Whittaker Chambers in gently rebuking William F. Buckley who was expressing concern about the potential demise of American Democracy stated very eloquently, "It is idle to talk about preventing the wreck of Western Civilization. It is already a wreck from within. That is why we can hope to do little more now than snatch a fingernail of a saint from the rack or a handful of ashes from the faggots, and bury them secretly in a flowerpot against the day, ages hence, when a few men begin again to dare to believe that there was once Something else, that Something else is thinkable and need some evidence of what it was, and the fortifying knowledge that there were those who, at the great nightfall, took loving thought to preserve the tokens of hope and truth." What a beautiful sentiment!

In closing out this segment I will briefly mention Socialism, a subject I will discuss in greater detail in the chapter concerning Communism. But suffice it to say, there is no Biblical basis whatsoever for Socialism either in the Old Testament or in the New Testament because of the simple fact that Socialism is totally at the opposite end of the spectrum of what it means to be a "God fearing person." People often say that Christianity is a form of socialism, but the Patriarchs, Prophets, Apostles and Jesus never taught this. They never claimed that the State had any obligation to help the people in need in this manner. It was always the individual, the community or the Church's responsibility to render help to the less fortunate. In fact Jesus spoke very forcefully about this matter. His Sermon on the Mount addressed the plight of the poor and less fortunate. He laid the responsibility of helping these people at the feet of the individual Christian. Likewise, His brother the Apostle James, spoke of proper religion being realized in ministering to the widow and the orphan.

Socialism and Communism and other forms of governments have altered the Biblical framework for helping each other. Now the faceless, heartless, bureaucratic state will dictate the means. Again quoting Reagan with his inimitable humor said of socialism, "Socialism only works in two places: Heaven where they don't need it and Hell where they already have it." He also declared "A socialist is someone who has read Lenin and Marx. An anti-socialist is someone who understands Lenin and Marx." Putting the pithy statements aside, it should be realized socialism has brought untold misery to hundreds of millions of people.

CHAPTER 14

———— ∞ ————

Communism

As far as ideologies directing the affairs of men are concerned, none match the Machiavalian madness of communism. The worst form of tyrannical government ever conjured by man according to Whittaker Chambers, himself a zealous communist for over twenty years before he became a Christian. His wonderfully and well crafted book "Witness" is must reading for anyone interested in how communism has infected and affected America.

Communism poses a revolutionary question asked since rebellious man was first endowed with free will: God or Man? If man's mind is indeed the decisive force in the universe as it is his wont to believe, why is God needed. Since the mental mutterings of a few social misfits in the eighteen hundreds gained traction by sundry means, the entire world has been in a titanic struggle. This has always been the case between good and evil, between people and nations who believe in God and those who do not. This is not a Manchian belief system between two opposing powerful Beings, one good, one evil, but the God of the universe and all creation allowing evil to flourish as a result of mankind's free will and rebellious nature. The great theological minds that predated Saint Augustine of Hippo and those who followed, especially of Reformed thinking outlined the tenants of man's fallen nature which echoed the magisterial Book of Romans authored by the incomparable Apostle Paul. God did not create a race of robots or autumontons, but human beings with free will of which He knew we would sin and infect all creation. In His omniscience, He had a plan to deal with this eventuality.

Karl Marx, the progenitor of Communism theory never worked a day in his life but had time to concoct and incubate this diabolism of communist thought. The man who penned the Communist manifesto did not lift his finger to provide for or feed his family which resulted in two of his children starving to death. However, the corpulent, louse infected taterdimilion ate his fill all the while being supported by Mr. Engles, himself the son of a wealthy free market merchant. Marx's family was so disfunctional, that two of his daughters, along with husbands all committed suicide at the same time.

This man was truly influenced by demonic forces which directed him to outline his idea of government and man's trajectory in the unfolding drama. His system of enslaving men's minds, creating endless autumontons has resulted in untold suffering, misery and death of hundreds of millions of people. Karl Marx was obsessed with Satan and used the writings of Charles Darwin with support from Engles and discontented others in his attempt to kill off God and religion. His poetry oozes his attachment to Satan with lines such as "This heaven I forfeited. I know it full well. My soul once true to God, is chosen for Hell." Or, "See this sword, this blood-dark sword, which stabs unerringly within my soul? Where did I get this sword? The Prince of Darkness. The Prince of Darkness sold it to me. The hellish vapors rise and fill the brain until my heart goes mad, until I go utterly insane." Indeed, this is chilling poetry. Paul Kengor an expert historian concerning the Cold War, wrote much about Karl Marx and his dance with the Devil. All the Communist such as Leon Trostky, Lenin, Stalin, Saul Alinsky and others wanted to burn and tear everything down starting with God and religion and ending with, the destruction of the family unit. A goal of these communists would be to rebuild society based on their utopian ideals. This consists of a multifaceted destruction of the core family unit. They turn husbands and wives against each other by means of manufactured issues. This system promotes abortion on demand as a form of family planning. Because of their anti-marriage and anti-family theories, a tremendous explosion of adultery, prostitution and illegitimate children occurred. Free love was encouraged with it's expected sequele. Doing your own thing we found can be quite harmful at times. The healthy Womens Movement has been co-opted by the communist agenda; it's intended purpose of neutering men in the process. Communism's "solution" for perceived and actual oppression and inequality amounts to the dumbing down of human morality all the while advocating for equity instead of equality. It appears we are all marching towards the same fate; destruction of our way of life in America.

Alinsky romanticized the drivel of communism even dedicating his book "Rules for Radicals" to "that first rebel who rebelled against God and won for himself his own kingdom, Lucifer." Of course, this book acts as a bible and guide for Leftists and radicals today with none other Hillary Clinton writing her college thesis concerning the book.

Karl Marx, this odious misanthrope hated people as much as he hated his own family. Even his father who converted from Judaism to Lutherism asked his son in a letter dated 1837, "That heart of your's son, what's troubling it? Is it governed by a demon? Is it governed by a Spirit? And is that Spirit heavenly or is it Faustian? This man so influenced by the Liberal Theology of Immanuel Kant and others has had an enormous impact on all mankind. All negative. Sending our children to public schools which are seeped in this nonsense is discouraging but I must remember that God is Sovereign and on His Throne directing all affairs towards the end of history and for His Glory.

Communists rule by brutality, intimidation and fear, there being many examples from history. Of course Joseph Stalin was one of the early purveyors of this evil. The Bolshevics were the first to fine tune the systematic killing of it's citizens teaching the finer points to none other than Adolph Hitler. The Halodormor famine engineered by Stalin against his Ukranian citizens resulted in a million Ukranian children being orphaned. To eliminate this embarrassment of children begging in the streets, Stalin ordered many as young as twelve years of age to be shot. Stalin was nothing if not a devilish beast.

The Soviet communist government was the first to establish concentration camps in the form of the Gulag system. Lenin established the first prison camp of this design in 1918 on an island off the coast of Northern Russia. By the time of Stalins death in 1953, there were more than thirty thousand such camps scattered across the Soviet empire. Alexander Solzhenitsyn the winner of the 1970 Nobel Prize in literature wrote of the horrors of these camps, many in which he had been incarcerated. Concentrations camps are usually thought to be a Nazi creation but the communists predated them by many years. The historian Viktor Suvorov documented and wrote about Hitler sending Gestapo officers to Russia to tour the camps and learn about their operations even before World War Two began. Nazism and Communism are two sides of the same evil coin and are often ruthless in dealing with their citizens they deem dangerous to the State. Despots regardless of the moniker placed upon them are all of the same DNA. They have an innate urge to control the affairs of others often using coercive and repressive means. Whether it's communism or fascism the goal is to control everything. The State is preeminent not the individual.

One must remember that Hitler and Stalin were allies at the beginning of World War Two. Their carving up of Poland and the terrible Katyn massacre of Polish officers and the intelligentsia in a Polish forest led to the subsequent betrayal of the non-aggression pact between Russia and Germany resulting in Stalin and Hitler becoming bitter enemies. There is no honor among thieves or blood thirsty rulers.

The only world leader at the time who understood the threat posed by communism was the inimitable Winston Churchill. At the end of the war President Harry Truman also began to understand the evil presented by Joseph Stalin. Churchill did not trust Stalin or any Bolshevis for that matter and spent the remainder of his life post World War Two educating all about it's danger. In 1946 he gave his famous "Iron Curtain" speech at Fulton, Missouri in the United States.

The Roosevelt administration was saddled throughout with communists sympathizers and spies throughout World War Two with avowed communist Algier Hiss firmly embedded in the State Department and was one of the President's most trusted adviser. In the famous photograph taken at the conference at Yalta, Russia, Hiss is seen to be standing directly behind a visibly ill Roosevelt. Of course, Stalin knew of all the inner workings of the United States government including the highly secret Manhatten Project tasked with developing the atomic and hydrogen bombs. A reluctant Whittiker Chambers along with his young lawyer Richard Nixon was instrumental in bringing indictments against Algier Hiss resulting in a Federal prison sentence. Whittaker Chambers designed an incredibly clever trap for the erudite Eastern Universities educated Algier Hiss. Hiss was a darling of the elites of academia, government, and Wall Street. It was going to be so easy to take down the frumpy, slow witted Chambers the erstwhile pumpkin farmer. But alas, Chambers who had a brilliant mind let Hiss continue to lie throughout the long trial before he sprang the pumpkin papers with reams of micro film proving Algier Hiss to be a bald faced Bolshevik liar. He had hidden the evidence in a pumpkin in a field of pumpkins which the communists were never able to find. The jury had no recourse but to reluctantly convict Hiss of treason and handing him a prison sentence.

As a side note, the historically maligned Senator Joseph McCarthy was correct in his diagnosis of the government being riddled with communists. Many people most uninformed, conflate and confuse Senator Joseph McCarthy's careful and sober investigation of Soviet spies in the government with the odious Congressional House Committee on UnAmerican Activities created in 1938 and lasting onwards to 1968 in which it was tasked with spying on American citizens exposing their political beliefs. This was very evident during the trials of Hollywood actors and directors. These trials devolved to the level of a witch hunt in contraposition to McCarthy's sober discoveries of sabatoge concerning our government. The Leftist press, academia and power brokers of all stripes have bent and shaped the narrative painting McCarthy in a bad light. However, at the time and in context, Joseph McCarthy was admired by the American people. At his funeral in Washington D.C. twenty thousand people turned out to honor the man. Ann Coulter has written extensively and accurately concerning this patriotic American.

The Chinese Communist Party has certainly been a quick study in the art of repressing it's own citizens. Brutal Mao Zedong first begin killing thousands of dissidents, intellectuals and anyone who he feared might be a threat to his nascent rule in 1949. The mandatory reading of his "Little Red Book" and the ensuing purges during his periodic "Great Leap Forward" programs resulted in tens of millions of innocent people being murdered. Of course, every tin pot communist dictator including Kim Il Sung, Pol Pot, Fidel Castro, Ho Chi Min, Hugo Chavez and others have all used these tactics. Communism is a terrible error that has been foisted upon mankind dwarfing all other forms of repression and in the number of suffering individuals.

Anyone who is an apologist for communism is an unhinged person. Leftist writers for the New York Times newspaper waxed glowingly about Papa Stalin in the nineteen fifties refusing to acknowledge his trail of atrocities. This has continued to the present day with many having a romantic idea concerning Socialism which Lenin himself huffed about describing Socialism as only a short stepping stone to communism. He actually called socialism as communism lite. As mentioned earlier, he also described Leftist as useful idiots, (his words) in helping to disseminate communism. People are always making excuses for the shortcomings of Socialism or Communism declaring they have never been properly executed with the promise that this time will be different. They always point to Sweden as the example of a shining socialism. However, Sweden is not socialistic but a people choosing Social Security as it's means of governance. They willingly choose to pay a very high tax rate in exchange for the State taking care of most of their needs from birth to death. This is different from Autocrats confiscating people's wealth against their wishes and then distributing it to whatever they deem is in vogue and best for the people. They rule with unbridled hubris. Margaret Thatcher the wonderful Prime Minister of Great Britan succinctly summed up Socialism as "It's a great system until you run out of other peoples money." Therein lies the great weakness of Socialism and Communism, they are both unsustainable. The ideas sound lofty and wonderful but in practice neither achieves any lasting positive successes.

Communism and Socialism are an existential threat to our form of Democracy. It has been a long slog beginning with at least the idealistic President Woodrow Wilson and his stillbirthed League of Nations. He appointed many avowed humanists in his administration with the very influential John Dewey leading the Department of Education. Dewey felt strongly that the State and not the parents should control education at the Federal level. The government should decide what children learn, leaving little leeway for parental involvment. This model has slowly and relentlessly indoctrinated our children at the expense of educating them. Of course, a powerful Teachers Union has been the machine behind this transformation. Now we have endless nonsense being delivered to our children in lieu of sound basic education.

Communist nations especially with China in mind, have a vested interest in seeing America dethroaned as the preeminent beacon of hope in the world. They have taken a long view and are patient in their efforts. Anything that will weaken us is good in their sight. Be it Tik Tok which young people in China have strict controls placed upon them because of the harmful effects but is widely encouraged in America, to the "silk road" initiatives, stealing of proprietary information, unfair trading practices, the military buildup and intimidation of their neighbors, are just a few of the tactics used. We on the other hand, are being lulled to sleep as we debate weighty issues such as "wokeism", transgenderism, reparations for people wronged, critical race theory, Black Lives Matter movement which is led by two Black communists women and on and on the list goes. I will discuss these issues in upcoming chapters.

The Left has weaponized many areas of the government such as the FBI, CDC, IRS, Homeland Securty and others in the attempt to muffle dissent. The FBI of which Whittaker Chambers warned about in 1946 is very much involved in the gathering of information concerning American citizens. He likened the agency to a police state similar to the Communist Soviet Union. Victor Dale Hansen writing in 2022 describes the FBI in terms of East Germany Stasi police in their handling of perceived political threats. Unfortunatly, weaponizing these agencies usually manned by life long bureaucrats portends poorly for the survival of our Republic as envisioned by our Founding Fathers.

We know that the first step in healing involves recognition that there is a problem. We need to wake up now. In reminiscence of the American university trained Japanese Admiral Yamamoto who devised the attack on Pearl Harbor of which he was against but nevertheless followed higher orders stated "once this is done we will have awakened a sleeping giant. Our end is sealed, it is just a matter of time." Even the revered Emperor Hirohito after the attack stated that this would be self destruction for Japan. They were indeed prescient; the end punctuated with two bombs, "Little Boy," and "Fat Man" the atomic and hydrogen bombs. We need to awaken from our slumber and unleash the might and goodness of America before it is too late.

The Communist specter has made intricate arrangements to destroy mankind and his freedoms. If we are to free ourselves from these devilish ideas, we must expose the conspiracy, identify it's fraudulant messaging and stop putting any hope in it's bankrupt creed. Civilization will again regain it's nobility when mankind recovers morality and virtue.

Leaving for now the more weighty subjects of Communism, Government and Hell, I will now turn towards a lighter more uplifting subject in the forthcoming chapter; dogs. As I have aged, my heart and soul have come to much appreciate this wonderful creature God has blessed us with and I would like to now share some of my thoughts on this subject.

CHAPTER 15

—ɯ—

Dogs

In this truncated chapter allow me to opine upon dogs. I have not always cared or thought much about dogs. They were just there. Often, I felt they were an unnecessary burden on everyone. Even as a child having a pet dog, a Doberman Pincer named Kurt, I never considered or thought much about him and certainly did not consider him a Lassie, a Rin Tin Tin or an Ole Yeller. He was just Kurt our bouncy playful dog who always stayed outdoors and was never well loved or allowed to enter our home. However, I thought it quite entertaining whenever the dog catcher pulled up to the front of our house and retrieving his net started chasing Kurt following his usual path going round and round his truck until Kurt tired of the game and sprinted away to safety under the shed in our back yard not to emerge until the catcher was gone. The entire episode had a rather cartoonish air about it.

My posture concerning dogs remained unchanged throughout my life even when I was married with two young children. This was the time when my life was spiraling out of control and a mixed breed Laborador female entered my life.

Banshee suffered the brunt of my neglect; always staying outside but ever obedient and loving. Years went by and she lying on her death bed taught me a valuable life lesson. Unable to rise, with me crying tears of conviction, she sought to comfort me with licks and paws. To the very end she was trying to comfort me. I realized at that moment dogs were special. I told her goodby, asked her for forgivness and returned to work as Jared my son accompanied by Janie, my wife, took her to her final vet visit. Jared carried her to a back room from whence she embarked on her final journey. Jared returning to Janie with tears in his eyes simply said, "It was harder than I thought it would be."

This was an Ebeneezer turning point for me concerning dogs. I vowed to do better, be a better stewart and a kinder master concerning dogs. Jared who has such a kind spirit told me "Dad, dogs just don't live long enough, they give us so much and then they are taken from us in just a few years." This I have realized is so very true.

Levi my next dog was a full blooded Chocolate Lab who everyone loved as he was kind to all he met. I have learned with some exceptions, dogs should be incorporated into the family unit spending much time indoors. They are pack animals and need and desire company. When Levi passed it was a sad day, but I had less guilt and remorse as I was a better friend to Levi. I was at work when the Vet called and said "I believe it is time." I went into a room so no one could see my tears. As each has departed they have taken a piece of my heart with them. Rudyard Kipling in his beautiful poem "Indian Hunter," asked the question "Why give our hearts to dogs? When they depart it tears our hearts." Be prepared to grieve when your own dog leaves you. Again Jared was tasked with taking Levi to his final vet visit. Levi was cremated and buried in a small casket in my wooded back yard attended by family members. It is amazing how an animal can capture our hearts so easily.

My appreciation and love of dogs has deepened as I have aged. I have come to view them as faithful friends; giving so much they expect little in return. They sense our many moods and will lie patiently awaiting our belated return then greet us exuberantly as if seeing us for the first time while never scolding us for being so late. At feeding time its like the best food they have ever eaten, thankful for our generosity in providing them with the same food year after year. My current dogs, Old Man Lab Louie and young whelp Labradoodle Luka have added so much to the chemistry of our family. I have grown protective and proud of my beloved companions.

The question is often asked, will dogs be in heaven? I don't know for sure and neither do learned theologians. We all have our own opinion on the matter; here is mine. Everything God created is good, therefore dogs are good. Dogs do not have souls and neither do angels as far as we can decipher from Scripture. Only humans have souls. Angels are in Heaven, why not dogs? They were in the Garden of Eden as Adam named them and they were important enough to be on Noahs Ark during the Flood. If they bring us such joy on earth, I would hope they might add to our joy in heaven.

Lord Byron's poem Braveheart and Robert Spencer's Gelert' Grave are two outstanding poems concerning dogs that I encourage you to read. The following two were written by me about my dogs Louie and Luka, and dogs in Heaven.

Wonderful Louie

Nothing grandiloquent about Louie
eyebrows frosted white
From little pup to old man Lab
how this dog my heart did grab
He is so comfortable at my feet
where he groans and moans on repeat
Gentle is he, patient with all
even with Luka when playing ball
Louie old man alpha, Luka the whelp
much to teach youngster with growls and yelps
Walking, pacing on vigilant patrol
no stranger into my abode will stroll
Ferocious bark, hackles on end,
only a fool would enter in
I know his heart the tenderest parts
the squirrls make a coward of him
but a copperhead snake, Louie defends then
venemous serpent now a has been
Oh how I love this wonderful beast
the best of man's friend, greater or least
He is my Greatheart written in lore
how I will weep when he enters death's door.

My Dogs

I am sure my dogs have no souls nor Angels I believe
but these curs so oft with better control than me.

My dogs most constant of my friends
another good gift our Maker sends.

Animals were in the first Garden, Adam named them all,
the lion, lamb in second garden as you may recall.

When content, quiet and near,
little for my friends to fear.

Even with thunders loud report
and other noise of this sort.

Heaven on earth where we will reside
mans best friend lying by his side.

God creates everything the good the very good,
not destroying His creation as many think He should.

Young dog puppy bounding at heart,
playing, encouraging me to take part.

My older Lab with fading eyes
content to contemplate paradise.

Wanting nothing more than smile, our hand,
matching mood to ours seeming to understand.

Lying both patiently wait
no rebuke if our hour be late.

These dogs they so comfort me,
stretching, moaning on repeat.

Older one, head resting on lap
talks to me as I doze and nap.

Louie and Luka I honor their worth
few matching or excelling here on earth.

Oh, I have bid some dogs farewell, soul rent in two.
it's a hard thing bidding such a friend adieu.

God is a God of good things my dogs are such a thing,
I believe in Heaven much joy they will bring.

CHAPTER 16

—⚜—

War

"War," a song by Edwin Starr is an counterculture anti-war anthem written in 1970 opening with the words "war, huh, yah, what is it good for-absolutly nothing." This song resonated with me at the time in my life as I embraced the counterculture, even flirting with the romantic ideas of communism. As I matured, it became evident to me that things are not always so simple. There are times when war is justified especially in response to some staggering evil.

It appears there is a constant war raging in the hearts of all people. As the reasons for war may be confusing, the only thing foggier than war itself is the exciting and frightening course to it's beginning. Following are the opening lines of a poem written by me expanding upon this notion.

> An ancient nasty little secret revealed,
> war is a seductress tempting and satiating the senses,
> concocting schemes, dashing men's dreams.
> Difficult for one to look away
> eyes fixed on the ones who lay slayed.
> Bones speak to other silent bleached bones,
> closing their eyes upon things of time,
> timing for them terribly unkind.

The antidote to this exciting siren call to arms is for one to receive the stripes and the injustice rather than meting out the stripes and possibly doing injustice.

In actuality, governments do not really fight wars at all but often start the conflict. This undertaking of fighting of course, is done usually only by men. Mothers will not send their sons to be martyred for mere politics, and few for hope of material gain or for money. Wars are always started by one man or a few privilaged with power but are always sustained, fought and bled by the mass of common man. The war could not be prosecuted unless a great number of men participated. If combat were left to a few old men to conduct, there would be few wars. What propels the common man to fight?

There can be many reasons for warring: lust or "need" for territory, a perceived injustice, alliances, religious differences and other causes, but one large reason is the person does not want his national home destroyed or his house changed. In truth, all people would rather be left alone with their familiar surrounding, family, friends and things they know. In essence their world. All people are like this; let me work, tend to my own business, my garden, my family and I shall be happy and fulfilled. People always desire peace. But if these things are threatened then it's not policy directing me now but something far higher, hatred. It's not love of country or patriotic zeal but hatred of unasked for or unwanted change. This is not a hatred driven by demons from hell but rather a righteous hatred driven by love. Love of home and hearth. Love of simplicity and calm of the familiar.

Man has been committing war in his heart since Cain murdered his brother Able as recorded in the book of Genesis in the Bible. Our hatred for our fellow man is just astounding. Of course, one of the earliest Commandments given by God to Moses enjoined us not to murder. However, Jesus as He so often did, takes it a step further in instructing us that anger towards our fellow man can at times devolve into a kind of murder in our hearts.

History is replete with examples of horrific battles which claimed many lives. One such early battle was recorded in Biblical writings concerning the battle of Mount Zemoraim in 913 BC. This clash pitted the kingdom of Judah led by king Jeroboam against the kingdom of Israel commanded by king Abijah I which resulted in about 500,000 slain Isralites and a victory for Judah. The number of dead in Judah's army is not given in the Biblical narrative but by any measure this was a hugh number of slain warriors not to mention the untold amount of injured people.

Much of a soldiers life is awaiting or preparing for battle. When the skirmish commences it is usually violent and over rather quickly but always surrounded by the ever attendant confusing fog of war involved. Usually combat will be of a small scale such as probing or even an accidental clash. Many times fear will destroy an army as men flee for their lives escaping their perceived deaths. There have been many times however, when the battle surpasses all normal expectations of war in it's scale and destruction. There are days when neither side is prepared to surrender or no escape is left open to them. At this moment these unfolding battles become epic in the history of warfare.

The battle of Gettysburg of 1863 left 46,000 dead on the field turning the Civil War in the Unions favor. In the battle of Cannae in 216 BC, Hannibal of Carthage destroyed the Roman army resulting in 60,000 dead. The first day of the clash at Somme in 1916 left 68,000 slain British and German soldiers with the battle of Verdun being even deadlier. Napoleon suffered his worst defeat at Leipzig in 1813 with forces losing 84,000 soldiers. However, the siege of Stalingrad in World War Two, which lasted for 5 months resulted in 1,917,000 deaths, a staggering number. There are many examples throughout history such as the Chinese Civil War which consumed many lives.

Mankind has always used every weapon he has ever invented, it's only a matter of time before it is used. An example is the use of the atomic and hydrogen bombs being used against a recalcitrant Japan in the waning days of World War Two. The use of those weapons stopped the insane war thus saving the lives of untold millions. The sacrifice of 200,000 Japanese civilians kept the home islands of Japan from being invaded and destroyed.

What a terribly difficult decision President Harry Truman had to make; sacrifice the few to save the many.

Any nuclear exchange in future wars boggles the mind in predicting the ensuing loss of human lives. In an all out nuclear exchange, mankind would be eliminated from the face of the earth due to the effects of the nuclear bombs and the inevitable ensuing years long nuclear winter. So much dust and debris would enter the atmosphere that all sunlight would be prevented from reaching the earth's surface therefore inhibiting photosynthesis. No plants would survive thus no food for animals resulting in nothing for people to consume.

We are all of the same fallen race of man and are prone to go astray and even attack other people. Some have steadfastly maintained a pacifist posture much like the peacful Quakers or the religious Moravians of Europe. But how about the rest of us? Can we at least have rules for conducting warfare that may limit the carnage. There are times of course, when one must defend themselves, family or nation. Fortunatly there have been men such as Saint Augustine of Hippo and later Saint Thomas Aquinas who gave us Just Rules for prosecuting a war.

Augustine was really the first person to offer a theory on war and justice. Cicero of Greece ruminated on the subject of wars, however, he never wrote a template with instructions such as did Augustine. Augustine used Scripture found in the Bible as his reference declaring some wars are justified to amend an evil. Thomas Aquinas refined and added to Augustine's rules. The Just War Theory is a set of rules outlining how to conduct military conflict. Following these principles would greatly limit potential strife.

Following are the stated principles:

1. it should be the last resort after all peaceful options have been exhausted.
2. legitimate authority; it cannot be waged by individuals but only by a legitimate authority.

3. just cause, it must be in response to a wrong inflicted. Self defense against an attacker is always justified.

4. probability of success, a nation cannot enter war with a hopeless cause.

5. right intention, the objective of a war is to re-establish an even better peace.

6. proportionality, the least amount of force should be used.

7. civilian casualities are only justified if they are unavoidable.

By following these reasonable rules much human misery could have been avoided. We need to see the enemy more like ourselves, more human. Wars might also be avoided if we could de-escalate negative thoughts about other people or nations, and treat them with respect while recognizing our own faults and times we have inflicted injustice. These steps might minimize conflict, but I fear war will always be part of the human journey.

However, at times man is capable of going beyond war and enters the realm of insane madness directing his steps to the neather regions of hell satiating his unrestrained evilness. The evils of man's unrestrained wantoness, savagery at times appears to be unchecked by the Great Restrainer, the Comforter of whom Jesus spoke. The Prophets, Patriarchs and New Testament writers spoke often of this innate condition of all mankind, his sin nature. Of course, all religions that people follow view man as innocent at his birth. They tend to stray away from this innocence and it is the job of religion to guide her in the right path. Christianity is totally different in it's view of man declaring all people are born with an inherent sin nature necessitating a redeemer for a corrective. This person of course is Jesus. People are trying to improve themselves enough to be accepted by a deity. But, we can never fix ourselves enough to be accepted, and by the way how would we know when we have been fixed enough. We need someone outside of ourselves to help us. Anyone who has been around a two year child readily can see how self centered and narcissistic they can be. No one need teach them, that is just who they are. These children require an outside influence in the form of parents, grandparents, grownups, siblings and others to guide them and set them upon the right path. The same with Grown-Ups. We need help if we are to stand before a Holy God. There is absolutely nothing we can do by way of "good works" to earn our entry into Heaven. But there is One who has paid the unbelivable price for our entry, Jesus Christ. This my friend is the unvarnished truth of the matter. If this maxim bothers you as it did me at one time, I suggest you read the Bible and take it up with God, the One who set the rules.

This defect in us is the fuel for the fires of Hell, directing some to pogroms and genocide. How can we so gibly look past ghettos as we go about our day? Gulags, concentration camps and mass murder on an industrial scale are things we would rather not think about or see. The systemic slaughter of Christian Armenians at the hand of the Young Turks of the Ottoman Empire leaving only 300,000 survivors out of a population of over four million is only a footnote if mentioned at all in our history books. Ukranians murdered, raped, starved to death and dismembered by the millions, four million to be more precise, by the likes of communist Joseph Stalin, Nazi's from Germany, Ukranian Quisalings among numerous psychopathic zealots from neighboring countries and ethnic enclaves. Even the Ukranians had a common enemy, the dreaded Jew. How ironic the Soviets, Russians, the Nazies and the Ukranians were all fiercly anti-semitic. Ukraine a part of Mother Russia allied itself with Germany in World War Two and fought against Stalin who had starved over a million of his citizens. It appears you reap what you sow with alligences and alliances which ebb and flow like the tide.

My point is this, war is terrible but inevitable. At least let us heed Saint Augustine's wisdom and try to mitigate the consequences of conflict. Beyond war is the rank evil which abides by no rules being rather directed by the basest demons from Hell. This is the history of mankind's sojourn upon this earth.

Paul the Apostle writing in the Book Of Romans in the Bible speaks to this in Chapter 1 verse 28-30. "And just as they did not see fit to acknowledge God any longer, God gave them over to a depraved mind, to do things which are not proper, being filled with all unrighteousness, wickedness, greed, evil, full of envy, murder, strife, deceit, malice; they are gossips, slanderes, haters of God, insolent, arrogant, boastful, inventors of evil, disobedient to parents, without understanding, untrustworthy, unloving, unmerciful." And rulers stood by and encouraged them giving their approval. Lord, indeed help us.

CHAPTER 17

---ﾕﾕﾕ---

Transgenderism

This is a strange subject to write about but it has risen to a hot button level of discussion in 2021 and even before that. Since man was created by God in the manner of man and woman throughout all of history, in every culture, tribe, tongue, ethnicity for all time have recognized the biological fact of only two genders, only two sexes, XX and XY, female and male He made them. No oops, no makeovers. I do believe the Apostle of Common Sense, G.K. Chesterton would have had much to say about this subject in his penetrating, incisive style. But again, he might be of the opinion as he did concerning his conclusions on philosophy and not accord it one hour's study. As the inimitable wit of Mark Twain would say, "there is truth, lies, and damned lies" and would forthwith place transsexualism in the latter category. I will rather quickly gloss over this crazy subject siding with Chesterton's sane advice concerning philosophy.

I will outline my thoughts on this growing societal ill. In forthcoming chapters I will avoid mincing any words concerning the malignant maneuverings of Progressives and Leftist on shaping a one sided discussion concerning Critical Race Theory, Marxist driven Black Lives Matters movement, Wokeism, power politics behind the Climate Change movement and other endless nonsensical drivil the Left keeps dredging up. But for now, I will start with transgenderism.

How did we get from common sense concerning biology to absurd sense? Ernest Hemingway when asked how one arrives at bankruptcy replied "gradually, then suddenly." The suddenly concerning transgenderism happened in 2006 in Java, Indonesia when trans activists, human rights professionals, dozens of United Nations rapporteures and committe members met and drafted a philosophic template for global policymakers to follow, and follow it they did.

Principle number three is pivotal in establishing the meme that trans women are truly women which flies in the face of all established biology. This toxic dust has settled on all our institutions infiltrating every nook and cranny of our legal, health, sports and cultural institutions.

It is also the principle behind de-coupling children from parental influence regarding discussions of sex education and the attendant dangers of hormonal therapies and sexual reassignment surgery. It allows men to compete as women in all women events even sharing showers, bathroom privileges and demanding to be transferred from men's prisons to women's prisons. Recently at a womens swimming competition a biological male presenting as a female won the event by an astounding 38 seconds ahead of the first real biological female. The spectators were outraged but their complaints were muted by the fear of being labled trans phobic. Even the vaunted Womens Movement only offers a stilted response against this convoluted worldview. Pressure by a very small group of very odd people has caused most sane people to cower lest they be labeled intolerant. Count me one who is intolerant of such foolishness.

Even Amnesty International which historically tasked itself with the noble endeavor of preserving prisoners rights has signed a letter drafted in Ireland seeking to strip people of political representation who do not believe in "affirmative medical care of transgendered people." What does that even mean? Once again it is Leftists inventing and defining new words or meanings in an effort to control the dialogue. Sane, resonable people lose the argument before it even starts. Words have meaning and people should be made to exactly define the meaning before any discussion. In doing so, they are forced to defend their arguments using the established meaning of a word thus often losing the arguments as all can see the convoluted reasoning and often outright dishonesty involved. The resonable commonsense person should become innured to the constant name calling, gaslighting and attached labels bandied about. For example, if everything happens to be labled racist, then in effect nothing is racist. The term loses it's power.

Since most people side with science proven normal biology, the mind boggles at such contrived nonsense. But people are bullied, vilified and harassed if they side with time proven science. This entire ideological house of cards is outrageous since it repudiates the most basic facts of evolutionary biology. There should be no place or quarter given for drag queen shows anywhere much less libraries or anyplace children are present. Parents who take their children to such places are doing much damage and in doing so are destigmatizing and normalizing the perversion.

Before modern society diminished religious faiths, the worlds moral order for all mankind had been stable for thousands of years. Morality was defined by God, not what people felt. Even nonbelievers and atheists recognized there was a moral order. Moral truth is thought by many today to reside within the individual. However, the Biblical narrative about truth is becoming more in conflict with societies view of truth.

Moral truth is grounded in the character of God; it is universal, objective and everlasting which is found in Scripture and the nature of God. The opposing societal view is based on a persons individual feelings resulting in subjective and situational results. People believe they know the truth through their experiences.

When we embrace Progressivism which is a form of Humanism, we are on the proverbial slippery slope to socialism or communism which are both very anti-God. So of course, most everything is accepted as long as it disrupts the Western values of a stable family led by a mother and father with a belief in God. The goal of the enlightened and progressive acolytes is to tear down and rebuild society in their new envisioned utopia.

There is no way to maintain our human dignity while ignoring the God given distinction between male and female. Male and female He made them in His image. We must be sensitive to the very real issue of gender dysphoria, it's been a recognized disorder for about one hundred years affecting 0.01 percent of the population most of whom are male. But, today it appears girls are manifesting the trait more commonly. Historically the little boys start evincing this dysphoria between two and four when he starts to identfy more comfortably as a girl. Good scientific studies have shown that when these children are left alone to navigate this time period without medical pressure to change or begin "social transition," about 70-80 percent outgrow the gender dysphoria. Most become gay men with some embracing transsexualism. However, they do not believe they are really women. It's just that they like to present themselves as females

Today these children are not left alone but are labeled trans kids by teachers and others. In schools, children have notions planted in them suggesting that gender is fluid and different from biological sex which of course is total nonsense. In many schools there is an systemic indoctrination in LGBTQ+ gender ideology where students imagine themselves as different genders; all eighty of them at last count. It has become so ridiculous now that it's morphed to the point that one can imagine themselves an animal or even a stone, acting with silly impunity in your make believe world.

Children who self identify as transgender can receive new names, pronouns, chemical blockers and actual mutilative genital surgery. This is often encouraged by teachers, therapists and doctors with little parental input or consent. California, New York, New Jersey, Colorado and Oregon all very liberal states are already far down this road. Insurers operating within the blessings of Obama Care or the Affordible Care Act are required to cover all medical costs. In Oregon, a child as young as 15 years of age can have everything done without parental knowledge or consent.

The Third Wave of feminism has stood silently by abrogating their responsibility of protecting womens rights. The few exceptions such as R.K. Rowling who speak against this nonsense is inundated with vitriol and death threats. The few honest researchers have great difficulty getting their research published in peer reviewed journals. It's as if the majority of sane people are being bullied into silence as they cower afraid they might offend the easily offended odd people.

This gender ideology is in many ways a sibling of Critical Race Theory. Both traffic in lies. The activists race hustlers want us to believe we should be defined by our skin tones which of course we fought a Civil War to overcome. The gender activists would have us believe there are untold numbers of genders that have the magical ability to change upon one's whims. Gender fluid is the new term that is now used. If we push back against Critical Race Theory we are labled racists. Resisting the idea of biological males participating in womens sports earns us the title of trans phobic bigots.

We are living in interesting times. The transsexual narrative has common sense turned on it's head. Eventhough boys manifest this dysphoria much more commonly than girls, there are more reported girls now believing they are indeed of a different gender. I feel this should come as no surprise as historically girls have been more prone to outbreaks of mass hysteria; and in a sense this current phenomenon has elements of hysteria. Of course, this will be argued against but there are many studies on girls and outbreaks of mass hysteria. It appears girls are more prone to this than are boys. The classical case was that of the Salem Witch Trials in the seventeen hundreds at which time a number of girls became agitated and hysterical accusing different people in the villages of being witches without any evidence but their feelings. Twenty eight innocent people lost their lives with some of them being burned alive at the stake and others hung from the gallows. There are many examples from history concerning mass hysteria such as in 1784 when a French nun living in a convent started to meow like a cat leading to all the nuns in the convent to meow as well. They would do this throughout the day and only ceased when the police intervened. Many such cases has occured in nunnerys and all girl schools. A more recent case in 1962 at a boarding school for girls in Kasaska, Tanzania resulted in 95 of 159 pupils laughing hysterically for hours with some laughing for as long as 16 days. It spread to other villages and schools. There are literary hundreds of examples, one as recently as 2019 in which this phenomenon has occured. The reason I point this out is recent research has found upwards of 30 percent of girls in some Eastern schools and colleges in the United States now identify as transgender, a staggering number considering only 0.01 of the population truly has a sexual dysphoria with most of these being males. Could this be a manifestation of mass hysteria? I believe this might be a manifestation in many cases.

I will remain sensitive to people with gender dysphoria but I will not lie and say transwomen are women. Men in spite of all they do to themselves can never really conceive and give birth to a baby. Obviously only a woman with her ovaries, ovum, fallopian tubes, uterus, placenta and birth canal with the exception of a cesarian section can give birth to a baby. It's always and forever only a woman.

Diabolical dark forces are encouraging this chaos with it's destructive objective of dividing the American people and destroying the core stable family. We must object to the indoctrination of our children concerning gender ideology. We must speak the truth in public and distinguish between usually wonderful transgendered people and the vile transgender movement.

CHAPTER 18

—⚏—

Wokeism, Climate Change, Critical Race Theory, Great Reset, Et Cetera

According to Friedrich Nietzsche, "Whoever fights monsters should see to it in the process he does not become a monster." In John Miltons "Paradise Lost," he outlines the evil trinity of Satan, Sin, and Death, helping us in the process to avoid becoming monsters. We must recognize the monster before we can transcend it. There are real monsters in the world, many birthed out of mans imagination. We imagine a perfect world where there is no inequality, no injustice and well tuned harmony. To achieve this we have conjured many monsters in the form of wokeism, the myth of man made climate change and other innane tropes.

Woke ideology does not flow from common sense experience or the lived experience of the worker class. There is a vast chasm separating the belief systems of the woke intellectuals and the common man and woman who actually work for a living. People who work and produce things really have no time left to engage and ruminate on this wacky nonsense.

Wokeism, the bastard child of socialism and leftism has weighed in on abolishing biology itself as we saw in the previous chapter. Today this deformed ideology is enamored with the number zero as it's ideal: Zero emmisions, zero covid, zero discrimination, zero economic growth, zero good humor, art and good sense. The woke tribe adopts all these tropes as a matter of group identity. This has become so preposterous only the privilaged elites and "highly educated" people could possibly believe it.

This offspring of leftism does not deal in reality. Everything from economics, gender fluidity to existential climate catastrophe, they believe in a fantasy that only the rich or privilaged can afford to believe. Whatever we read or wherever we go there is a constant bombardment on our senses of wokeism.

This is no small matter affecting even our military. I am sure our enemies have taken notice of our proclivity to embrace every odd ball whim thrown our way. According to Lieutenant General Thomas Spoehr, the greatest threat by far to our military fabric is the woke ideology promoted by progressives. Wokeism in the military is being imposed by elected and appointed leaders in the White House, Congress, and the Pentagon who have little understanding of the purpose, character, traditions and requirements of the institutions they are trying to change according to this General. What a tragic laughingstock we have become to a watching world. Now it is decreed that active members of the military can take time off from their duties to obtain gender mutilating surgery and all related hormone therapy at tax payer expense. What utter nonsense.

Of course Critical Race Theory is being "taught" to all military personel. These indoctrination programs are little more than Marxist propaganda. Books such as Ibram X Kendi's book "How to be antiracist" which is required reading for many in the Services contain statements such as "Capitalism is essentially racist" and that "truly to be antiracist you also have to be truly anticapitalist." It goes on and on with the Air Force creating "Barrier Analysis Working Groups" with eight being identified such as "Indigenous Nations Equality Teams" and the "Lesbianism, Gay, Bisexual, Transgender, Queer or Questioning Initiatives Team."

Not to be outdone in the dance of stupidity, wokeism also comes in the guise of conflating the mission of the military with environmental ideology. The Joint Chief of Staff stated the greatest threat to America is global warming. When I was a young man in the sixties and seventies our extinguishment would come in the form of an Ice Age. It appears we cannot make our minds up. I mean you can't make this nonsense up as our nation state enemies laugh at us. This craziness along with drag queen story hour at military bases must come to a halt. The faithful and good people of the military should still receive our honor and praise for what they are doing in protecting this great nation. However, addelbrained leaders must be replaced.

Critical Race Theory will now be mandated for all to follow in an effort to excise racism and discrimination by viola, embracing racism and discrimination. Forget wonderfully gifted and out of date Doctor Martin Luther King who railed against the very idea of racism and bigotry based on skin tones in lieu of one's character. The great battles of the Civil War and the great toil in obtaining Civil Rights Laws will now be abrogated by vapid reasoning of over educated proponents of another itteration of slavery.

Teaching revisionist history is not the answer to any of our questions. Certainly teaching about our history of slavery in America must be taught and explored and this has been done. Great progress has been made in race relations and more work is to be done. But to claim we have made little progress and we remain a racist nation is disingenious. Our progress is amazing testified to by our Black President, Supreme Court Justices, Blacks in every strata of America's fabric. White privilage and institutional racism do still exist but are being exposed and ferreted out. Pitting one group of people against another is not the answer and we must be careful in our temptation to follow this path. Even our leaders at times have fallen into this trap.

Leaving the topic of race for now, I will discuss the idea of the "Great Reset" which has burst upon the scene seemingly out of nowhere. Leftests and Progressives have an unusual skill at wordsmithing. The common decent person is always at a disadvantage forever playing catch-up to the ever changing cascade of words. Elitists trained in elite schools either consciously or unconsciously follow the Marxists rules for radicals. They attain positions of power and influence as middle or upper level non-elected bureaucrats. Then we have the super elites such as the jet sitting Davos Switzerland group populated by United Nations apparatakes, titans of tech. Big Pharma, unelected government officials, the press and education establishments all dictating the same message to the world; "This is what we have decided the new order will be."

Klaus Schwab founder and chairman of the World Economic Forum published a book titled "Covid19; The Great Reset," which defines the reset as a "means of addressing the wokeness of capitalism." They have redefined classical capitalism as "neoliberalism" and pits it against the new "Stakeholder Capitalism." This new system entails the marriage of corporate cooperation with the State which would vastly increase governmental interaction in the economy. A function of woke ideology is to encourage the majority of people in developed countries to feel guilty about their wealth which the elites aim to reset downwards; except of course for the elites themselves who need to be rich allowing them to fly to Davos each year in their private jets spewing tons of carbon into the environment. The rest of us, G.K. Chesteron's common man, has to endure "organized loneliness," Hannah Arendy's term which encompasses a global view of mankind. This is manifested by compulsory lockdowns, masking, social distancing, and social exclusion of the unvaccinated. None of these has any scientific facts behind them but this does not dissuade those in power from forcing these mandates. In following and allowing these measures to go unchallenged, we cede more control to a selected few. We indeed are compliantly giving away our self-identity, self-worth and self-actualization while meekly laying down our hard fought freedoms at the altar of the elites. We should be inspired by the high ideals of our Founding Fathers. The real challenge and danger to America comes from within.

The alien philosophies throughout the long and often tragic slough of history of the world are always the exalting of governments directing the affairs of a subservient citizenry. In summary, the American philosophy is liberty for the individual; the alien philosophy is tyranny. As these are an antithesis, they cannot co-exist. As James Madison the author of the Second Amendment which ensures the protection of the First Amendment stated that "The truth is that all men having power ought to be mistrusted." Again quoting the inimitable G.K. Chesteron from his wonderful book Heretics of 1905 stated "Fires will be kindled to testify that two and two make four. Swords will be drawn to prove that leaves are green in the Summer. The great march of mental destruction will go on. Everything will be denied. Everything will become a creed."

In defense of their evil work, modern curators of wokeness use positive terminology such as "justice," "democracy," "homeland," "popular government" and the like to justify their agendas. There is little so toxic to mankind than the power to govern. We should never concentrate power in the hands of anyone or any group no matter how kind or benevolent they appear. So many philosophers and students of human nature know the proclivities of man. People are not equipped to handle absolute power no matter how kind and pleasant they appear to be. Who would have dreamed an Adolph Hitler sitting in the Vienna Academy of Fine Arts would in twenty years morph into a devil? Few are in number who can walk away from the intoxicating elixer of power. The peerless George Washington leaps to the fore in this small cadre of individuals.

Who lurks beneath these demonic masks of power? The local school board and zoning committee control freaks, people speaking of "packing the courts," and other maneuverings designed to keep people agitated with their "new ideas," confusing language sowing chaos and complexity come to mind. We should look to the State for nothing more than law and order. The State is even having great trouble in controlling orderly legal immigration. A nation without defined borders quickly denigrates to a Balkanized situation.

I would now like to opine upon the "Green New Deal," and man made climate change. There is little as maddening as this nonsense which is driving our great nation backwards towards a Luddite mentality. It appears the greatest nation to ever grace this earth is hellbent on self destruction. There are a number of examples I will mention.

The frothy fetish to electrify our vehicles is surreal. Of course these require lithium batteries which are very expensive to manufacture. Mining the lithium and disposing of used batteries is very difficult. It requires five hundred tons of earth to be mined to produce one ton of lithium. Thirty square miles of the Atacama desert in Chile has been turned into a brine lake by pumping fresh water from the aquifer which is sorely needed by the indigenous people. After evaporation, the material is then shipped to China by diesel powered ships for processing. Indigenous peoples, other citizens and the environment suffer greatly. It cost approximately two hundred thousand dollars to produce twenty car batteries each weighing about one thousand pounds. These are enough batteries to supply twenty Tesla electric vehicles. In comparison, one barrel of oil at ninety dollars will produce more energy than all twenty batteries. The very idea that our electrical grid which at times is already overburdened will be able to accommodate millions of vehicles recharging at all hours of the day or night is preposterous. Where is the extra electricity coming from? Since wind and solar generation are so affected by weather, their two percent contributation is laughable. In reality, which is an uncomfortable place for leftists, the extra electricity will of course be produced by coal fired plants, natural gas, hydroelectric and nuclear power. America has at least five hundred years of coal, two to three hundred years of already proven oil and gas reserves. Our country has the largest known repository of energy in the entire world, but the Green New Deal is still being pushed on the hapless American citizens. We spend trillions of dollars on this scam while studies show that this type of energy production still accounts for less than one percent of the worldwide energy needs. It is interesting that burning wood still provides more energy than all the solar panels in the world. Just the mundane practical matter of forty million apartment dwellers in America having to recharge their car batteries while parked on the street is not well thought out. However, wealthy elites among us are smug in their confidence of charging their battery while parked safely in their garages, or even at Whole Food markets while shopping organic, never thinking upon the fact that all the product in the store was made possible by fossil fueled trucks maintaining the supply chain. We are indeed living in a "Mad Hatter" world of the Green New Deal. It appears that progressives don't even consider that gas and diesel powered farm equipment and ranch equipment make it possible to produce the food in the first place.

America is the number one producer of oil and gas in the world surpassing Saudi Arabia and Russia in spite of concerted efforts to destroy this energy sector. How is it beneficial for us to ask other usually hostile nations to ship us more oil and gas which necessitates shipping costs with it's attendant increased pollution footprint while we could easily increase our own cleaner production. Reason and common sense is woefully lacking in the Green New Deal zealot's minds.

Drinking the Kool-Aid of the Green agenda we are told will automatically end "climate change" caused by man. We must dispense with common sense and ignore the vast resources bestowed upon America in the form of oil, gas, and coal. For our energy needs we will now invest trillions of dollars in hawking this pipe dream. A by-product of this will be new regulations forced upon us by these little Czars as the golden age of wind and batteries drifts down upon us.

We have not well thought out the many problems of transitioning to green energy such as the senescence of the equipment. A comedic irony is that a small wind turbine requires about twenty one gallons of oil equivalent to half a barrel of oil for it to operate. This oil is used to lubricate the gear box and requires regular monitoring and maintenance for proper function of the wind turbine. Of course, there is a cost to this that few are willing to discuss.

The hugh wind turbines have a life expectancy of about twenty five to thirty years before becoming inoperable. At todays dollar, each turbine cost about one million dollars to purchase and construct. However, it is estimated it will require about one million dollars to dismantel the equipment when it comes to the end of it's useful life. Who is going to pay for this and how to dispose of the materials which are not easily reuseable? One can envision acres of wind farm ghost towns.

The same with high tech lithium batteries at the end of their useful life. This material is dangerous and very difficult to recycle safely. Most recycling stations will not accept lithium batteries. The explosion and fire hazard is just too great. But I am sure we feel smug and superior as we motor about in our electric vehicles. The bottom line is gas and highly filtered coal power plants remain the best source of energy for America.

Vast amounts of pollution is contributed by communist China and Russia with large additions by India. Europe and America are much more responsible in the handling of gas, oil and coal. Nuclear power accounts for more than half of Frances needs and is a very safe and pollution free source of energy. The design of modern nuclear power plants are quite advanced with the likelihood of accidents remote. Besides, we know the risks of nuclear power but not so much the consequences of wind or solar generation.

There is much more that could be written upon this subject such as the fact that our entire national fabric is grounded upon petrochemicals from asphalt for our highways, pharmaceuticals, plastics, transportation, food production, a mighty military, high tech and low tech jobs which all depend on oil. But for now I am going to turn my attention to our nation; the wonderful nation of the United States of America.

CHAPTER 19

——✺——

America

The central story of America is not being told or taught, only our flaws are highlighted at the expense of all the good America stands for. Even with our many flaws it is still a pretty good story. It should not be a Valentine story that's presented but an honest rendering of the entire narrative of goodness and badness that is America's history.

What does it mean to be an America citizen? How is a young person able to go forth into the world if they do not have a strong sense of what it means to an American? It appears history teachers and professors have forgotten their primary purpose in teaching history.

Teaching this subject is not so much about telling what has happened in the world as it is about explaining how the world came to be what it is today. How despite our overpreening self-righteousness, there is little difference between our humanity and the humanity of others who went before us centuries or even millenia prior. We are just as flawed humans today as our ancestors thousands of years ago were.

Teachers should be there to help connect the dots while encouraging the students to not leave with any sense of superiority. They need to leave asking the questions; compared to what? Comparing America to a perfect paragon, a standard of unexcelled virtue is a standard that will always fail. But if compared to the receptivity of legal immigration, and standards of foundational freedoms, America does excel. People are desperate to come here in spite of our shortcomings of racism etc. because of one thing, hope. This is a land of hopes and dreams and possibilities.

However, instead of having a sweetness about our story, children are being taught only about slavery, Indian displacement, Japanese internment camps, climate change and how evil and greedy we are as a nation. People are shocked when learning for the first time that slavery for example has been the typical rule across human history instead of the exception. The problem it appears is due to history teachers and others focusing for the past thirty or forty years only on social history at the expense of political, diplomatic, constitutional and military history.

We should be careful for what we wish for. We have entered a time of awakening, unfortunately not of the kind of the Reformation or Puritans Great Awakenings. This is an awakening of "wokeness" which was covered earlier. Our "elites" in Academia, Wall Street Titans, heroes of the Sports World and Tech Gurus have bestowed upon America their vision of an alternative universe. All have boarded the woke train to ferret out perceived or actual grievances such as "White Rage" and privilege for example while employing legions of "diversity, equity and inclusion" czars. This harkens back to the utopia envisioned by the founders of communism. These pinched faced nattering nabobs of negativity have nothing to add to the vibrancy of America while attempting to pit one group against another.

Leftists have a propensity to change language because they operate in a virtual theoretical world. Since they cannot abide by words with specific meaning, they create euphemisms and gaslight as they navigate their dystopian world. A recession as always defined by two consecutive quarters of negative growth is now known as a "complex" recovery. Words are concocted to make something evil sound good such as "political correctness" which is never good. It is a term used to suggest only those on the Left spectrum have the correct view of politics. "Identity politics" is only a euphemism for "tribalism." They also endorse the absurd ideas that we can self identify against scientifically known facts concerning gender, race and biology.

Left wing feminists pushed to have secretaries rebranded as "executive assistants." Unions pushed to have janitors retitled as "custodial engineers." The Left appears to be more concerned about symbolism than reality. Self determination is now championed over scientific facts for political purposes resulting in divisive demographic tribes. An example that was explored more extensively in the previous chapter is that of gender which for all time has been determined by obvious biology and more recently by DNA and not by what one feels or desires. This is somewhat similar to the famous story proposed by Abraham Lincoln when he asked; "if you consider the tail of a dog as a leg, how many legs does the dog have?" Many peoples answer is five when in fact the dog really has only four legs. A tail is not a leg just because you may call it that. The purpose of language is clarity not confusion or controversy.

The attack upon language by the Left is very purposeful. By giving a word a new meaning it creates angst and confusion which is the purpose of the exercise. This leads to chaos and unease with people now longing to return to safer and more recognizable times. This desire of people for stability is often satisfied by elite leftist leaders. A Benito Mussolini had the trains running on time, Adolph Hitler brought efficiency and Joseph Stalin brutal order.

Another tactic used by Progressives is to redefine history by declaring there are different versions of history. Actually, there is only one history, the thing that happened, be it a Pearl Harbor attack by the Japanese starting World War Two for America or the example of slavery. There might be different interpretations of what caused the event but only one true actual event. Unless being cautious many people will start to believe the lie and minimize any pushback against the now new paradigm. As Mark Twain said, "A lie goes around the world before the truth ever get's it's pants on." However, these falsehoods are easily debunked by insisting the Left define the words they are using. The contortions and gymnastics in their effort to sound rational are laughable and easily exposed.

What does it mean to be a progressive, a wonderfully sounding word? Proper English would tell us it might describe making something better, more wholesome, better habits, upholding family values or any other positive descripters. But this term has been co-opted and turned on it's head as is usually done by Leftists and others groups of their ilk. How pray tell is open borders progressive? Tearing down statutes and sculptures of national heroes while rewriting American history is not progressive. Redefining marriage contrary to Natural Law, calling riots and looting "peaceful protests," the term progressive becomes awkward. Bigoted racial theory, medical tyranny and conglomerates becoming wealthy at the expense of smaller businesses and defunding law enforcement should not be celebrated as progressive. I believe most Americans would rather call this regressive thinking. We should respect our English language and it's honesty. We must use words correctly without attaching a new meaning.

There are so many things from my perspective to address concerning the ills affecting and infecting the soul of America. Some have already been noted however, there are a few more I would like to briefly explore. This certainly appears to be a pessimistic drumbeat I am playing, but there is light at the end of this tunnel. For now I will quickly address the topics of crime, monetary policy, addictions, relative truth, equality for all, education and finally the American Revolution as compared to the French Revolution.

Crime is now seen as a construct to protect the elite with their prerogatives, privileges and property. Thuggery, shoplifting and looting now appear to just be part of the scenery of those who live in a city. Forget that people everywhere want a structured society. In many places one can now steal up to one thousand dollars per incident with little fear of punishment. This is a result of progressive district attorneys and state attorneys refusing to enforce the laws already on the books dealing with this problem. However, please stay far away from our palatial homes guarded by gates and fencing and guards. This I believe is mindboggling nonsense.

"Social Justice Warriors," which in itself is a nauseating self promoting title they mantle themselves with, will now defund the police while they provide protection. Remove bail requirements, the threat of incarceration and mandatory jail time and viola, people will magically start to behave themselves except in the real world they don't. History and the Bible teach there must be consequences for one's egregious behavior. Now granted, the fairness of the meted out consequences have often been unfairly distributed between the poor, the privileged Whites and everyone else. To remedy this injustice requires us to be true and steadfast in upholding the laws, not dismantling them to a level of anarchy. We can learn this lesson by studying the French Revolution of 1789. In an effort to overturn stifling overburdensome laws, the young zealots pushed the pendulum too far to one side resulting in chaos and death.

Modern monetary theorists assure us they have finally solved the scourage of inflation; this to be solved by simply printing more money. Forget about the teachings of Friedrich Hayek from 1899, or Adam Smith even earlier. Lets play the game involving capitalists with too much money being forced by market place manipulations and outright confiscation now forced to give their money to the needy who unfairly have too little. This form of Socialism history tells us, never works. However, these modern day alchemists will now properly teach us the overlooked nuances of this beautiful new system.

We are also in some respects a nation controlled by addictions. This is a wealthy nation, a place of leisure with time on our hands. Without being well grounded in the proper virtues or the wisdom of Solomon, we can become self focused, shallow, pleasure seeking, ill informed and poorly educated narcissists.

Addiction is a complex phenomenon. Condescending and peering down upon the heroine addict or alcoholic we may fail to see our own addictions. We just know we are better and stronger than the cocaine user. However, our desire for a momentary dopamine flush of an emotional high may be enhanced by binging on carbohydrates, sugars while all the while feeling good about ourselves as we strive for a higher plane. We can also eat green and lean get a good feeling while riding our Peleton, become a gym rat, starve ourselves, run for miles or a variety of other activities we can do as we dance with our acceptable addictions Adrenalin junkies in reality are not much fun to be around.

The more subtle and widespread of our addictions can come in the guise of new phones, games, cars, houses, fads, things to do, places to go. Anything for a momentary dopamine high as we strive to avoid thinking upon the more difficult things. Big Tech, Wall Street and Madison Avenue become our respectable dealers. This is a pox upon our country and will need to be soberly addressed and solved or these addictions will lead to our demise.

The American border remains porous inviting millions of unvaccinated, unvetted illegal aliens to flood into our country. A popular television commercial depicts Jesus as "one of us," He gets us, He was also an refugee. This feels good and sounds good but it is far from the truth. Jesus was a citizen of the country of Judah and was actuality born in Bethlehem. People are so easily swayed by false information. A nation which cannot control it's borders will eventually lose it's identity, becoming not a melting pot but an unrecognizable mosaic of people groups who Balkanize themselves into tightly defended tribal groups. The only thing left to Americans is the right to vote. However, undocumented people we find are now voting. This bodes ill for this nation.

Identification required for voting is relentlessly fought against in America by Leftists and others of their kind who claim it will disenfranchise the less advantaged. However, forty six of the forty seven nations in Europe have very strict voting laws with most requiring photo identification, a thumb print and various other identifiers before allowing a person to cast their vote. None allow mail in ballots, few allow absentee ballots and none allow ballot harvesting. Most Americans are modest and conservative and would never elect these radical Leftists if the elections were actually fair. However, wealthy individuals and foundations have cleverly manipulated the elections allowing those with harmful agendas to be elected. This all becomes clear upon a little investigation. Instead of disenfranchising people, when they realize the elections are actually fair as in Europe, the percentage of people voting rises significantly. They finally believe their votes really count. The votes are usually counted rather quickly usually within hours of being cast and not like the farcical methods dreamed up in our nation.

Our befallen and broken education system has consistently failed our students. Unless a student is enrolled in a private school or a charter school there is little chance they will be exposed to a classical liberal education. The Teachers Unions have a stranglehold upon the system and are very resistant to any encroachment on their power. There is often chaos in the classroom with little respect extended to the teachers. Inner city schools at times resemble a war zone with students showing total distain for what's happening. The parents want their children to obtain a good education as do the students but it is not available. The amount of money spent on each student is among the highest in the world but the end result is frustration and illiterate children. The teachers union makes sure there are plenty of principles, assistant principles, layer upon layer of administrators, little czars of all stripes but no real attention given to the student unless provided by a caring, kind teacher. It is not the teachers fault, it is the corrupt and broken system.

The system is geared to consistently overemphasize the negatives while underemphasizing the positive aspects of our nations history. This tends to hollow out the standards of the educational system which sets the denominator at the lowest level. It appears for example, the slave trade will be discussed while negating any real discussion concerning the

Constitution or the heroic William Wilberforces of the world; mostly old white men who thundered against the vile practice resulting eventually in it's demise. A return to a civic-centric methodology of teaching concerning our founding, our Constitution and what it means to be an American may not cure our soul but it would be a soothing balm for what is ailing us.

Millions of children remain enrolled in public schools that continually teach revisionist history which is weighted against America; Ronald Reagan's "Shining City on a Hill." An example stated earlier is the toxic critical race theory birthed out of the 1960's. The Marxist agenda behind this and the Black Lives Matter movements requires that personal identity must first be revealed followed by a nations exposed history and codified values replaced by a new Marxist communist agenda.

After the 1964 Civil Rights Act became law, there was great angst and upheaval in the Black community because of an identity crisis; they had been defined by White oppression. Instead of the expected gratitude, many Blacks raged against the now guilty and embarrassed Whites for putting them in this situation.

Critical race theorists and Black Lives Matter activists now look to reparations for relief and frame their arguments in philosophic terms of justification. This obviously will not work. We all should be pursuing radical forgiveness and recognize that race alone cannot be one's mark of standard. Culture, the American culture, should be the touchstone binding common traits and beliefs, customs and traditions. We have so much more in common than we have differences.

Removing monuments and symbols that offend us is not the answer. This is part of our history and they should be preserved if for nothing more than to study it and become better people. A time proven tactic of despots is to first remove any remembrances of the past and it's peoples' history while directing attention to revisionist history as taught by the "new leaders." If this is allowed to continue we will be one generation removed from knowing who we are, where did we come from, and where are we going. Our ancestors are at times disrespected, elders set aside and mocked in society as the woke unwise youth lead the entire parade. A nation then dies as it loses it's ancient footing and traditions.

The great experiment unfolding before us is one where progressive regression is stripping away the institutions and methodologies of the past which defines our civilization. When Americans struggle under high inflation, street violence, unaffordable fuel, rampant illegal immigration and a weakened military we will long for that very thin veneer of civilization. What lies beneath this veneer is utterly terrifying.

All advances in science, medicine, food production, arts, and the rare gift of leisure have happened because we are civilized. However, the rub lies in this observation; this leisure has made us arrogant. We take this leisure as our birthright as we forego hard truths and reasoning.

We just need to remember the great Greek city-states, the Roman empire, Renaissance Republics and the European democracies before they all imploded.

Relative truth and theological relativism in our nation today is similar to the six blind men touching different parts of the elephant believing they understood completely the whole by only examining part of the animal. Very much like today when we are talking past each other convinced of our righteness. We refuse or do not want to see the other side of the argument. Truth becomes relative, your truth as opposed to seeing the absolute truth. God's Truth.

Knowledge puffeth up as the Apostle puts it. A man does not have knowledge as he ought and he so very proud of the little he actually has. We see such a small part of the large we should forever stay in a humble state. This hubris of man also leads to theological relativism; again the relative truth which fits so comfortably into the worlds wisdom. In reality, the six blind men with a little exploring could have more closely approached the truth of the matter, a magnificent animal the elephant.

A common ploy used by Progressives is demanding equity for all. This noble desire is often used as a tactic to divide people pitting them against one another. This primary goal is to divide and distract the American family. This is quite evident in the feminist movement where women are encouraged to remove themselves from the traditional roles of primary care givers and protectors of the family to now being employed themselves in the workforce.

This often results in confused roles and many times adds stress to the family. Two people are now needed to work in order to pay for the extra cost of day care, the need for two cars and other necessities now required to support two people working. The lie promulgated to promote this misadventure is that quality time is as important as quantity time spent with the children. This lie is now exposed for what it is, it is a balm to assuage the guilt of the parents in spending less time with the children especially during their formative years. Children need and desire a parent being with them even if the parent is not interacting with the child at all times. The child wants the ministry of presence of the parent, be it boring or exciting times. They just want to know the parent is at home. Men being let off the hook of providing for their families has at times abrogated his responsibilities, in effect becoming an absent father. Many families are now matriarchal in structure. We can all see the effect of a failed family structure. This is right out of the communists playbook. The links between feminism and socialism are easily seen.

Alexis de Tocquerville said in 1848; "Democracy and Socialism have nothing in common but one word, equality. But notice the difference; while democracy seeks equality in liberty, socialism seeks equality in restraint and servitude."

"Most arts have produced miracles while the art of government has produced nothing but monsters." The man who spoke those words was twenty six year old Louis Saint-Just, an architect and enforcer of the French Revolution. He was one of the founders and visionaries of this revolution along with Maximilien Robespierre. They designed, directed and excited the masses of French people in the intoxicating names of "Liberte', Egalite', and Fraternite'." These noble words enflamed people to commence six weeks of beheadings and hangings resulting in literally rivers of blood running in the streets. At the hight of this blood sport, it is estimated over ten thousand people a day were executed in France before both Robespierre and Saint-Just themselves fell victim to the guillotine in 1794.

This revolution was in no way as noble as it is usually depicted. The country to this day has not completely recovered. In comparison to the American Revolution of 1776, the French Revolution produced nothing but bloodshed, death and failure. This in contrast to the American Revolution of 1776 which resulted in many magnificent wonderments. The glorious document such as the Bill Of Rights, the Constitution which have not only given us a template for how to govern but others also. Obviously it's wonderful precepts are still being worked out but the goal still is for life, liberty and the pursuit of happiness. We have this sense of hope for the masses as this "Shining City on a Hill" acts as a lighthouse of kaleidoscopic light for all to see.

Thank God for Lafayette the "father of two revolutions." He admired and so loved America more than those of his native home of France. A brilliant man who loved liberty, he joined the American Revolution at age nineteen and fought valiantly for our freedoms. His life was filled with amazements as he navigated through fifty years of intrigue all the while avoiding the guillotine, rebuffing King Louis the eighth and Bonaparte Napoleon eventually being rescued by President James Madison who brought him back to his adopted, beloved America, the greatest of liberties. He penned the framework document which became the French declaration of freedoms.

As I bring this section to a close, there are a number of antidotes that I believe might start to heal this staggering Nation. The most important is to reclaim our educational system which has over the last seventy five years been slowly hijacked by well intentioned socialists. The very powerful teachers unions must be brought to account. A true classical liberal teaching agenda should be encouraged. The great art of teaching instead of the craven act of indoctrination should be the goal. When people are truly taught the wonderful history of America, they will start becoming proud of their heritage instead of being apologists. Of course, our country is fraught with errors and blemishes but these should be discussed and debated. The dialog must not be shut down by casting shame or intimidation. True vigorous ideas can stand on their own if given the chance. As Saint Augustine said, "truth is like a lion chained, release it and it can defend itself."

There are lessons we can glean from history where this very thing occurred. I remember as a twelve year old boy the Hungarian Revolution when hundreds of thousands of mostly young people rose in unison against government totalitarianism. This revolution lasted for a few exciting, hopeful weeks before the always brutal Soviets crushed it. Over two thousand were killed and more than two hundred thousand fled to the West.

After a grueling day at work, these parents would go home and silently teach their children about religion, history and culture. Since Hungarians historically had a close attachment to Western values, it became an effective counterbalance to Marxist propaganda. Students began to be able to see through the lies they had been exposed to in the state schools. This should give us hope. But we must realize the communist education system ultimately failed only because the familial education system succeeded. All parents at every level of the system, public, private, and the collegiate must strive in preparing and raising a generation of young people who will stay true to values and principles of previous generations. This commitment is far more important than the quality of a governor or a school board in the raising of a child.

In this climate of a fractured America, it is easy for one to become jaded and discouraged. The moral decline and the civil coarseness along with the educational decline are not inevitable. There are enough good citizens to stanch the bleeding and begin turning the State ship around.

When I see young people performing choral works of liturgical beauty in Latin for an hour, or volunteering to help in sundry ways, or planting a vast farmland using immense combines before ever having a license to drive a vehicle on the highway, or an inner city youth overcoming, an elderly Black person with joy in their hearts, people helping the disadvantaged get basic sewage disposal rights for the poor in Alabama, or the millions of unspoken saints doing their works in the shadows, my heart is humbled and I become joyous in my hope for a better nation.

Tyranny, you don't know us and lawlessness you will never speak for us. America with all of our imperfections is still the brightest beacon the world has ever seen. This the grandest experiment concerning the affairs of man, dispensing hope to mankind while showcasing the most breathtaking of freedoms we have ever witnessed.

Every generation before us has had these freedoms threatened as every generation rose to defend against. It is now our turn at the helm. Our enemy is now more insidious, wrapping itself in deceit while declaring patriotism is a worn out idea. They would topple this nation in a heartbeat if they could. However, liberty still stirs our souls and we will defend our blessings for our children while magnificent America remains standing.

CHAPTER 20

~~~

American Black Eyes

Much has been written about the maltreatment of Indigenous people, American slavery and the shameful mistreatment of Japanese Americans during World War Two. Voluminous informative materiel about the American Indian has been written with some bad and good conclusions being reached. There is little disagreement the Indigenous peoples were maltreated, but much has been romanticized about this subject. The white Europeans for certain are very aggressive people descending from Hun, Visgoth, Vandal, Viking, Celtic, and Briton stocks. These people were and are quite war like and if left unchecked will overrun other people groups. Indigenous people occupying North America for thousands of years had made very little progress as measured against European standards. So of course, they were easily over taken and set aside. This does not make it right but it is the truth.

Historically there are many examples of this happening from ancient times to the present. The Cro-Magnon man, Neanderthal man being overtaken by more modern people groups. Ethnic Serbians overrun and displaced by Croatians and the ongoing extinction of native Amazonian tribes, Caribbean Island peoples and pressure placed on many African natives come to mind. So this was not a new phenomenon concerning the American Indian and should be placed in proper historical context. To reiterate, I am not excusing this abominable practice but only trying to describe it accurately.

The American Indians, just as white Europeans and all others of the world enslaved each other. All nations and people accepted and viewed it as a good business practice. The worlds economy was powered by slavery. The Iroquoise indians fought and enslaved the Hurons and the Mohicans enslaved the Algonquian indians. The Canadian tribes fought and enslaved each other as did most American tribes. The Mescalaro Apaches battled and made slaves of the Mexicans and American white settlers. They also attacked Comanches, Kiowas and all others in their areas. So no one should feel their group is superior to another group in this regard. As pointed out earlier, mankind has been abusing each other for thousands of years. The Irish, Scots and English are still at times acting rather ugly towards one another. The Russians and Ukranians and the communist Chinese and Uyghurs are even today in a death match.

The American Indian was often romanticized by the European and Eastern American press as a "noble savage." However, the more accurate truth was the American Indian brave was not much different from a young white male who had time on their hands which often times led them into trouble. These young people are prone to mischief and often times can be bullies. Roaming around looking for excitement or an advantage many times led them to trouble.

Moving forward to the present time and in proper context, todays aimless youth often gravitate to their own kind be it gangs or cliques. Their kind understands them and accepts them. Over time as they mature their world view hopefully expands as they accept and are accepted into the larger society. Obviously, eventhough there are differences there are also many similarities between early Twentieth Century Irish gangs, current hood gangs, Tammany Hall gangs, Klu Klux Klan gangs and Indigenous gangs. The need for recognition, power and influence is a desire in all of us and if left unchecked and unfettered invariably leads to baser traits we all possess.

In reality, American Indians were not much better caretakers of their environment than were others. Often they would camp or settle in an area until it became despoiled by human waste with the surrounding area depleted of food resources. At this point they would be forced to move to a new location. Thousands of bison were slaughtered in the quest to ensure a few as a food source for the tribe. These animals were often driven over cliffs into ravines or canyons while only a few were claimed.

They lived close to their environment and understood it well but that does not necessarily translate to better caretakers. Many of the indigenous people groups lived a subsistence existence with hunger and starvation always a pressing claim. An example is the now extinct Karankawa people who lived along the Texas coast near swamps and estuaries. The very name Karankawa is a derisive moniker given to them by various tribes. The name means dung eaters and these hapless people scavenged whatever they could find including the dung of animals. These poor people were looked on with distain.

Many tribes as we know depended on a single major food source such as the American Bison placing them at a high risk if this supply was disrupted; and disrupt the European settlers did. The White settlers, Mexicans and even the Indians so decimated the herds that.it placed great stress upon the Native Americans.

Learning the nuances of European duplicitous negotiations, the settlers so easily lied to the Indians going as far as reneging on the proffered promises of relocation. Even American Presidents were dishonest with the believing Indians, so of course they were eventually overrun and subdued. This remains a terrible black eye on America. Even today The American Indian often struggles as the rest of America hums along.

Of course, Christianity has been faulted for polluting the "purer" Indian belief systems. Much has been written about this, most sympathizing with this view, however, a wonderful book, "Light in a Dark Continent" gives a different perspective. This land in reality was inhabited by darker forces holding captive and sway a pagan people. The fact of the matter is that early Friars and Priests along with very early Evangelicals arrived on this land bringing with them the Light of the Gospel of Jesus Christ.

These Franciscan and Jesuit missionaries helped people resist worshipping pagan entities. Christ's Church will always bring Light into every dark area exposing evil. It is impossible for darkness to overcome light, light always overcomes darkness. Of course, this is a very unpopular position to hold, but the only one I believe will stand the test of time. I am compelled to at least broach this truth as uncomfortable as it may be. Because of these bold missionaries many of the lost souls were led to the Beauty of Christ and have been added to the multicolored fabric of Heaven.

Turning our attention now to another black mark upon American history, I will briefly discuss the internment of Japanese Americans during World War Two. This is certainly a very large black eye on America as the Democratic Party initiated and ushered in this terrible action. Placing the situation in historical context, the Democrat administration of Franklin Roosevelt was concerned that the law abiding hard working Japanese American citizens would side with and pay allegiance to their historical home of Japan. This fear never translated into action as the loyal Japanese continued to work and tend to the many small businesses they owned and in fact, many enlisted into the services to fight for America and against Japan.

Innocent people were rounded up and placed in these internment camps which were located throughout America. These in no way or manner should be compared to the concentration camps being employed in Nazie Germany or the Soviet Gulags. These German and Russian camps were slave camps and places of mass executions with none of these horrid events taking place in the internment camps. However, this still remains a terrible injustice suffered by our fellow citizens and denizens of this nation of which we should all be ashamed. Trying not to cast too much blame on one party since there is much to go around, it appears much of the misery and poor decision making resided with the Democrat party. Issues such as supporting the institution of slavery in the South, formation of the Klu Klux Klan organization, implementation of Jim Crow laws, the encouragement of share crop farming-a form of indentured service, the constant undermining of Reconstruction efforts after the Civil War, with most members voting against Civil Right laws of the nineteen sixties with even a Democrat President Lyndon Johnson using racial slurs in describing African Americans were championed by the Democrat Party. In contradistinction, the Republican Party was first formed in Wisconsin just prior to the Civil War with it's sole platform demanding the abolishment of slavery. The very first presidential contender was none other than the incredible, initimable Abrahan Lincoln.

The Republican Party fought for reconstruction efforts, fought against the KKK, Jim Crow laws, share cropping practices among other evils. All these examples were resisted by the Democrat Party who only started backing the changes when it became politically advantageous. They quickly maneuvered and got out in front of the parade as if they were indeed always leading the efforts. But a point in fact was that most African Americans voted Republican with this starting to change only in the late 1960' when the Democrats co-opted the Republican narrative and stance. Taking a page right from Joseph Goebbels playbook the Nazie darling, they begin repeating lies until people started believing them. The Republican Party then became the perceived racists in peoples minds. These detestable lies have lasted to the very present times. It appears the Left fetishizes race and ethnicity. It has enshrined the idea of "good racial discrimination" in an effort to stop racial bias which in effect forces us to be racially biased. People are basically lazy and do not want or care to really think or study history, being content to be led about by "elitists" who will tell them what to think and what to do. George Orwell's 1982 comes to mind with it's "double speak" and Animal Farm where all are equal but with some being more equal than all others, that being the pigs. What interesting times we live in. However, history is replete with such nonsense as Plato stated, "Strange times are these in which we live when old and young are taught falsehoods in school. And the person that dares to tell the truth is called at once a lunatic and fool."

"When men choose not to believe in God, they do not thereafter believe in nothing; they then become capable of believing in anything. When the Divine is forgotten or thrust aside, civilization is doomed, dreams become nightmares and the world goes mad." These words of G.K. Chesterton should forever ring in our ears.

The modern Left is overrun with people who believe any number of unseen or impossible things. The Left in fact is a very religious group by temperament, but lacking any real faith in God. This makes them like any religious people in any age, they can be vicious and intolerant of anything they perceive as heresy. They have persuaded themselves, many younger people and generally the less educated among us that climate change for example is an existential threat to human survival.

However, the more immediate existential threat of abortion and coerced family planning is glossed over or not talked about at all. These Leftists are more comfortable in their world of fantasy sans facts or statistics. One would think that if there was such a thing as gender fluidity archeologists would long ago have found more than just two genders, male and female in their painstaking excavations. Again, there are no third, fourth, or fifth options in the farmyard or the archeology digs. These godless mystics are the useful idiots who are easily manipulated by willing hard line activists who; for the most, are not very pleasant people. No reasonable persuasion will bring them to their senses but over time reality with it's harsh lessons will sober them and bring them to heel. But much suffering which might have been avoided will unfortunately occur.

CHAPTER 21

Music and Poetry

Music is well said to be the speech of angels. Nothing among the utterances of man comes closer to the Divine as we approach the infinite. Music touches every sense we possess while we experience our emotions. Some compositions are so haunting and ethereal simultaneously, leading us to reflection, questioning and inspiration which coalesces into a wonderment of the moment. As Ludwig von Beethoven mused, "Music is a higher revelation than all wisdom and philosophy." This is as true a statement as his opining that "There are thousands of princes in the world but only one Beethoven." The unspeakable language of music in uncovering deep emotions and understanding surpasses that of any efforts of sages or philosophers. To be moved by a musical composition upon hearing it is to experience the highest intellectual state.

Listening to the many Ava Maria's that have been composed from the lovely Franz Schubert's classic that many millions have so loved, to the more recent composition by Franz Biell with the score truly touching the heavens is a testament to what Beethoven was saying. Different from the Ava Maria's is the recent composition by Sir Karl Jenkins the Scottish composer who combined his stunning Benidictus with the awe inspiring God pictures of the universe opened to us by the Hubble telescope. You must listen and see what this genius has composed and in doing so you will on bended knee be humbled. I believe with all my heart the most precious gifts we can receive is life itself, love and beautiful music.

There are so many things wrong in this world we live in. So often there appears to be little hope and only despair on the horizon, but hearing such wonderful music fills one with hope. What is it about music that stirs the emotions? Like all beautiful things it is a gift from the Lord; not to be studied, parsed and figured out, but just to rest in it's goodness.

Great music has the ability to make a grown man cry as he reflects upon his life of lost opportunities, friends and loved ones. We should stand in awe and wonderment with open arms embracing these wonderful creators of such music. This, the sound of angels weeping with joy.

I play the piano and enjoy classical pieces especially those composed by Haydn, Mozart, Beethoven, Schubert and Chopin. Music to me for so long was a love hate relationship. My concentration was on technique at the expense of the music in my efforts to avoid wrong notes, almost holding my breath as I approached a particularly difficult passage. I would awkwardly stop playing and muddle my way through the section never really taking the time or effort to correct the mess. This went on for many years and was quite frustrating for me and annoying for anyone listening. This was my modus operandi for many years while never really understanding the musicality of the piece. Two things occurred which were correctives. The first was I started taking lessons from a wonderful lady at age fifty five. My wife Janie introduced me to Mary Anderson who started teaching me about proper fingering, timing, music theory and other basics stretching me in the process far beyond what I thought possible. The other freeing moment for me came as an epiphany after reading a story about Beethoven and his young lady student. The story unfolds thusly.

Giving a young lady her lesson, he had her play a sonata. As she played he stepped to the window and appeared to be lost in thoughts. Perturbed at seemingly not being listened to, she started playing dissonant notes and chords. When Beethoven continued his reverie she in a sudden huff ceased playing. This triggered Beethoven's attention and approaching the young lady inquired of her as to why she had stopped playing. Answering she said it appears you care not that I play wrong notes, so why try. The answer given by the immortal Beethoven changed how I approached playing the piano. He told his young student "there are no wrong notes just music and the beautiful silence between the notes." This answer astonished me which now allowed me to be free to play through the "wrong" notes and just enjoy the musicality of the piece.

A more recent episode along similar lines involved the famed jazz pianist Herbie Hancock relating a story about him striking an obvious wrong chord while performing with legendary musician Miles Davis. As soon as he struck the wrong chord, Davis improvised picking up the wrong chord and inserted it into the now new rendition of the music. This startled Hancock and at the end of the set he asked Miles about it. Davis replied that it was an opportunity to explore new music. Improvisational fusion jazz was born out of such "mishaps." Miles stated "If you hit a wrong note, it's the next note that you play that determines if it's good or bad." This indeed is freeing information for those of us who play.

There are so many wonderfully gifted composers and we all have our favorites. My five are Joseph Haydn, Amadeus Mozart, Ludwig von Beethoven, Franz Schubert, and Frederic Chopin, each attaining this pantheon for varying reasons. Other great composers have captured my imagination such as Franz Listz, Felix Mendelssohn, Peter Tchaikovsky, Sergey Rachmaninoff, C.P.E. Bach and most recently the aforementioned Sir Karl Jenkins. Then there is my third tier which I am sure will be disputed by others but this would include pretty much everybody else with the exception of Richard Wagner the antisemitic who I find boring, and pedantic. I truly cannot listen to him. Knowing others more gifted than I place J.S. Bach as a preeminent composer but little of his music transposes me. Schoensberg, Stravinsky, Mahler and others of their ilk will be left to be appreciated by others more insightful and learned than I.

But, let me for a few moments concentrate my thoughts upon my favorite five starting chronologically with Joseph Haydn who was firmly planted in the Classical tradition. He was a prolific composer producing in excess of six hundred pieces, one hundred and six being symphonies.

Papa Haydn as he was affectionately called is still refreshing to listen to and still seems so original two hundred and fifty years later. He admired and was influenced by C.P.E. Bach the second son of J.S. Bach, the same Bach that Mozart and Beethoven so loved.

Joseph Haydn in turn taught Mozart and Beethoven the art of counterpoint in their compositions which allowed them to greatly expand their music. Haydn was instrumental in developing chamber music and is known as "The Father of the Symphony" and the string quartet. He was an honorable man befitting the times of the Enlightenment age and at his death at age seventy seven was credited with enormous accomplishments and influences.

Amadeus Mozart was a good friend of Haydn learning much from him. They had great respect for each other and often performed together. Despite his truncated time upon this earth, passing at the young age of thirty five, Amadeus was a prolific composer who traveled in the realm of genius. During the Classical period he produced over eight hundred pieces spanning many genres such as symphonic, concerto, and the operatic repertoire. He is by all measures one of the top three composers who is admired for his melodic beauty, elegance and richness of harmonies. He evinced prodigeous ability and was composing and performing at age five traveling throughout his life gleaning insights from various composers.

Viewing the human voice as the greatest of instruments, he went on to write many rule bending operas. The female coloratura soprano was his favorite. Listening to the high clarity of this soprano voice in the aria, "Queen of the Night" is breathtakingly astonishing. Haydn writing of Mozart said of him "posterity will not see such a talent again in one hundred years," and telling Mozart's father "I tell you before God, and as an honest man, your son is the greatest composer known to me by person and reput." One is left wondering, what great compositions and ability followed Mozart to his early grave.

My favorite composer is the incomparable, mysterious, brooding Ludwig von Beethoven who in my humble opinion is a rare genius. I love Mozart but I stand in awe of Beethoven. None approaches his ethereally stupendous music with the possible exception of Franz Schubert in his later works.

Beethoven is just Beethoven, an enigmatic genius who overcame terrible obstacles including of course his well known deafness. He bridged the Classical era as he dominated the Romantic period until his death at age fifty six in Vienna Austria.

A relative new appreciation of mine is the late discovered works of the diminutive in stature only of the tragic Franz Schubert. He was discovered posthumously to be a towering figure who adored Mozart and Beethoven. He was so poor that he relied upon the generosity of his fellow artists and his brother. He could not afford his own piano until the last year of his life. Very few of his works were published during his lifetime. He died at the age of thirty one in his mothers arms and is now recognized for his deep emotional feelings exhibited in his compositions. Much of his work lay undiscovered until after his death, Felix Mendelssohn, Robert Schumann, Franz Liszt and Johannes Brahms along with Schubert's brother discovered his vast oeuvre and championed the performances of his compositions. He is now considered one of the greatest composers of all time.

Frederic Chopin the wonderful Polish composer and virtuoso pianist rounds out my top five. He wrote during the Romantic period and some would argue that none equaled his compositions for the piano. His nocturns and concerti are stunning in their beauty and poetic melodies.

Now let me seque into poetry, a favorite medium of mine. I started writing poetry about the age of seventy two after being inspired by a dream. I have grown to admire and love this genera. I do wish this interest in poetry was instilled in me at a young age. As a school boy, Winston Churchill memorized all one thousand two hundred lines of

McCauley's "Lays of Ancient Rome." I am sure his love of poetry inspired and encouraged his later renowned oratorical skills.

Poetry is unique. It is one of humanities most treasured art form. Writing poetry can offer us a unique way of expressing our thoughts, feelings and memories. There is evidence both poetry and music can awaken our brains, bringing experiential joy. This medium connects people at a level that is far deeper than linear thinking can do. There is almost something sacred and mystical about poetic words. Poetry acts as an interior flame that inspires us in times of stress many years after we have learned the lines.

Learning some poetry by heart with it's rhythms and images is like a muscle that grows stronger as it beats in our hearts and is life-giving until the end of our days. Music is well said to be the speech of angels, but poetry reveals their hearts.

CHAPTER 22

─⁓ ⋙ ⁓─

Growing Older

Aging or ageing if your British, is what will happen to all of us if we live long enough. We will all get older. As I near the end of my life, I am more aware that I am over the "drop zone" and the bay doors might open at any time releasing me to my fate. In effect, I am on borrowed time as we all are from the moment of our birth to our final demise. It has taken me most of my life to really start to understand this fact. At times I thought I was rather large but in reality I was quite small. Me thinking I had a soaring intellect but in actuality not having any deep thoughts at all. Thinking I knew so much about life but it was life's illusions I knew best. Sublime at times is the dominion of the mind over the body, in effect letting the weak become so mighty.

As I grow older, I realize I know so very little. The great Socrates as he was given the cup of hemlock to drink was asked "what do you know?" His answer is profound to me, "I know nothing." This is a truth we should all dwell upon. Shakespeare's writing stated, "A fool believes himself wise, a wise man believes himself a fool." As Scripture teaches, the world's wisdom leads to death. The only true wisdom is dispensed by God. We should all slow down and ponder this truth.

It is true that many with an unbearable trembling realize that in a sense they have been dead long before their appointed time to die. These people have mistaken life as nothing but vanity. Having all and being all, at death they realized they have failed. At this moment for them, the physical life may actually be a spiritual death instead of physical death now ushering in a spiritual life. Our attitude towards life should form our attitude and acceptance towards death, even if it necessitates us running the gauntlet from terror to triumph. Ignoring or denying death is delusional and only encourages fear, frustration and superficiality.

By accepting death, this allows us to be more confident with attended contentment and calmness. Though death may eclipse the trials and concerns of life, love lives on for all time and eternity with a life of it's own. The challenge for us as death rattles it's bony doors is to remember that living well allows us to die well. Death shrinks into insignificance as the life well lived thunders with confidence. The wise and wonderful Puritans all believed we would do better and be more content if we spent more time contemplating our coming death and the wonders of Heaven. There are a number of poems I have written about ageing and I would like to share them with you now:

Tending to Totter

Tending to totter as I age
not desiring of turning the page.
Mind directing walk straight this way,
walking enfeebled tending to stray.

Standing quickly a risk I take
afraid now this head I brake
No glory in aging quite like this
going about my day I persist.

Amazing it is time always wins,
reminded that's how its always been.
No matter how the story is spun,
this age narrative has always won.

Doddering, tottering old man fool?
I could learn much attending his school.
Experience of life connecting the dots,
this wise old mans knowledge is sought.

When seeing one totter weakened by age
extend your hand steady this sage.
In Gods beneficent wonderful plan,
in grace one day you might stand.

Death Fog

We are wired in a most peculiar way,
knowing we will die, but just not today.

We go about our day as if death does not exist,
its on the back burner in a fog and a mist.

It appears to me a marvelous thing
sans fear of death being not on display.

Of course, we all know this is a ruse,
death happens to others, us it won't bruise.

This distraction is healthy if not taken too far,
each person functions like a miniature czar.

Healthy and normal this being okay,
allowing us to function as we tend to our day.

Knowing at times death comes into view,
sobering, anchoring us for a moment or two.

Being made like this is good and right,
otherwise all day we would die of fright.

The biology, genetics, tellomers sublime,
Creator has measured and marked out our time.

Don't fixate on what can't be fixed,
enjoy your time in this skit of skits.

Between our birth and our ending, life happens to us with each life having the certainty of uniqueness. Some lives are spectacular for sundry reasons, most are rather mundane and some wretchedly dismal. Many emotions, experiences and feelings are shared by all on this human journey. Of all the feelings and emotions, the universal one that stands out is grief.

Grief is a very individual experience yet also a universal reality for all of us. We will all at some point lose something very dear to us which will impact who we are and our underlying understanding of the world. While grief can be horribly painful, it also has the ability to lead us to a deeper understanding of all things. We can more deeply appreciate life and the living of it. The reverse side of grief is love, this enigmatic wonderful cosmic alchemy. We really only grieve the things we deeply love. To deeply grieve one must have deeply loved.

As Henri Matisee the renowned French painter remarked, "The pain passes but the beauty remains." If I were to lose a son, instead of saying "I am so sorry for you," I would hope someone might say "I loved him so much." William Shakespeare tells us "Give sorrow words; the grief that does not speak knits up our wrought heart and bids it break."

There is a vast repository of wisdom and knowledge stored in the entire process of aging. Youth with it's tightness and tautness, it's lusts and vigor passes rather quickly, but like a hound refreshed by the scent, age overtakes. It's of a sudden when the epiphany pushes it's way to the fore; I just realized I am getting older. My lusty, youthful vim like a vapor has vanished. Now begins a lifetime of tapping the brakes so to speak, trying to slow the looming juggernaut coming for me. My body starts to rebel and sag. We are forced to come to terms with our new reality. Once thinking hubriscally that this would never happen to me, I am now faced with the fact I am not so special after all.

So much has been written about youth and the beauty of young women; why can we not awaken to the beauty of an old woman? The Lord gives us blessings and mercies many times over, but the blessing of an old mother for us only once. We should tenderly revere her and maintain her in our hearts, for when gone, she is never to be replaced.

The Roman philosopher Cato, reasoned old age appeared to sit heavily upon people because of their decreased active pursuits, a weakened body, the deprivation of physical pleasures and impending death. However, he stated "My old age sits light upon me, and not only is it not burdensome, but it makes me happy." Cato had his reasons as I have mine; an appreciation of beauty, not actively raising children any longer and not needing to work at a job. I can enjoy coffee with my beloved Janie as we sit on the porch watching the sunset or sunrise and marvel at the varied birds going about their business, having a drink and wonder at the changing seasons with their sundry colors. I enjoy people more and the beauty that sits upon them.

As the body slows and many obligations fall away, we who are older may have the time to enjoy and absorb the vast panorama surrounding us. I find myself spending more time on the porch or near to the fire pit with friends watching the birds, squirrels, plants and clouds. My senses are more aware of the varied breezes moving about me as I marvel at natures pageantry and the stunning kleidoscope of Gods creation.

My grandchildren bring me pure pleasure either in real time or in my storehouse of memories. I also take pleasure in other peoples children or the myriad of people I meet everywhere I go. Gods marvelous creatures.

In aging, I realize most troubles are mere trifles. There are things of vital significance in my life: the health and welfare of my children and grandchildren, my friends and even my beloved country. However, most troubles fail to enrage or sorrow me as I grow older. They lose their importance and urgency.

I am more grateful now. Gratitude is surely one of the graces bestowed on me as I age. Just rising in the mornings reminds me to thank God. I have more time to pursue my passions, whether writing, painting a landscape, playing or composing for the piano, gardening or just being with good friends.

When sickness or death of a friend comes, it can be quite difficult to cope, but this is part of life. The key is not to let pain and sadness keep us down. My prayer is that all could age well or at least develop a spirit of acceptance and keep moving forward to our appointed end.

CHAPTER 23

—⁓—

Closing Remarks

My simple advice and insights are gleaned from seventy eight years of living with some snippets mined from here or there such as the simple ways of the Amish community. Nothing profound was expounded upon but only good sense which has survived for eons of time and found in many varied civilized cultures. It still amazes me how vaunted man so easily stumbles.

Not being automontons or robots but a creature made in the Imago Dei with free will, we began to make many wrong choices early. In the beginning the Lord gave man only one law to obey; "Don't eat of this one tree but you can eat from all the others." Adam and Eve could not keep this one simple rule and they ate of the forbidden tree. Well, this turned out poorly for them and for all people thereafter.

God then said I will now give you ten laws to follow- the Decalogue or Ten Commandments. Everyone of us has failed this test everyday and usually in spectacular ways. We all at sometime will have malice towards others. Envy, greed, murder (gossip), adultery (lust), resides in our hearts daily. At some point man started adding more laws ostensibly to help us better control ourselves. The Pharisees were notorious in adding six hundred thirty two laws directing the affairs of man. Of course, no one could possibly adhere to these sometimes quirky statutes which led Jesus to declare that they had placed a very heavy burden or yoke upon all. His solution was to simplify to only two laws; Love your God with all your heart, mind and soul with the second being like the first, love your neighbor as you love yourself. Needless to say, we are constantly failing even this simple rule. By intimately knowing and loving Jesus we at least have a better chance of being more Christ like in our approach to life.

So in closing is my simple advice. Don't use foul language, or curse which only reveals the dearth of your language skills. When competing in games try to be an honest winner and a gracious loser. Say your sorry if you have injured another physically or with unkind words. Don't blame others for your mistakes, keep yourself clean and wash your hands. Share and give a helping hand. Don't expect others to do what you can do for yourself, Speak life into people not death. Get married and stop playing house, and don't experiment with drugs.

Be intentional about what you let into your life. Facebook, Snapchat, Twitter, Tik Tok and endless other social media platforms are enormous time wasters having very little upside. This social addiction I fear will be viewed by future generations as a great experiment that went terribly wrong. Our time would be much better spent with family, gardening, learning a skill, writing, playing games, fellow shipping with friends, reading or just being quietly present with yourself and God.

We might choose to stay home more rather than going to another social event. Our celebrations might become simpler. Being satisfied with less is an admirable goal. Learn the "Golden Rule:" do unto others as you would have them do unto you. Live life with an open hand and not a closed fist. Avoid extremes, living moderately beneath your means. Volunteer your time and talents. Feed the hungry and homeless.

Putting first things first makes common sense such as faith, family and friends. The Amish are far from perfect but they provide a touchstone for me. My faith is important, my friends stopping by for a visit is important. A son calling me by phone will never be placed second on my list as it is of the highest priority. Grandchildren calling or stopping by, this I cherish. When all is said and done these are the things that will be remembered.

As mentioned earlier, I have learned to be more grateful as gratitude has been bestowed upon me. Just getting through each day relatively unscathed is a grace. The times we are actually scathed is a time for humility knowing how blessed I really am.

Gratitude is the fuel that should propel us. This gift is often found and nurtured; in a tender place of tension; living in the moment while striving for our future. Gratitude calls us to a higher place, it pushes us to see the beauty in the right now, better than the easier path of complaining and comparing both of which accomplish little. Our tender space has room enough for our dreams and emotions while never shaming or foresaking us. It conditions our hearts to be humble, patient and persistent. At times it is so easy to feel the full weight of disappointment, wishing things might have turned out differently. Getting mired in the muck is easy, it's often what I know best, and like an old jacket it fits. But, at this moment I must nudge myself to really feel my emotions of disappointment and acknowledge the weight while wishing for a better outcome.

It is okay to feel sad and at the same moment yearn for a better future. Gratitude is the healing balm balancing tenderly the tension of past, present and future. As I live my wonderous life, I am learning to never bemoan or compare but just be in the tenderest of places, the now.

There is much in this book that might lead you to believe that mine is a Christian view and your insight would be correct. I truly and strongly believe that God our Creator has given us all the means, knowledge and wisdom to do what is good and right but because of our fallen nature and our free will, we have horribly failed. This book I hope has nudged us to think more clearly and cogently concerning many subjects that now bedevil us. Whether we agree or not, there is only one Truth and that is the person of Jesus Christ. There are no other gods besides the Holy Trinity-one God, one essence, three persons. Other religious gods are nothing more than counterfeit and frauds.

Johnathan Edwards the greatest of American theologians wrote hundreds of years ago that Satan has trained in the best divinity school in the universe. This demon is a master of counterfeit and lies who opposes

God at every turn. God, the giver of life, Satan the taker of life. God speaks only truth, Satan only lies. God loves, Satan hates and on and on it goes. So of course we can become confused and disoriented. This simple book humbly highlights a few of our struggles and I pray it might help us in our journey.

Thinking Straight is a book I hope might encourage and at the same time provoke you to think and revisit your world view. Many subjects are explored and the reader will quickly discern my bias; a Christian Western world view bias. I would hope this would not dissuade people who hold other faith based views. There is much common ground we tread upon as we collectively push back against the current wave of nonsense. I must confess, a small part of me hopes this book becomes controversial. We should hold hands with common sense our guide as we wade into the fray.

Printed in the United States
by Baker & Taylor Publisher Services